FINANCIAL REPORTING IN THE EXTRACTIVE INDUSTRIES

ACCOUNTING
RESEARCH
STUDY NO. 11

FINANCIAL REPORTING IN THE EXTRACTIVE INDUSTRIES

By Robert E. Field, MBA, CPA
Partner
Price Waterhouse & Co.

Published by the
American Institute of Certified Public Accountants, Inc.
666 Fifth Avenue   New York, New York   10019

Copyright 1969 by the
American Institute of Certified Public Accountants, Inc.
666 Fifth Avenue, New York, N. Y. 10019

Publication of this study by the American Institute of Certified Public Accountants does not in any way constitute official endorsement or approval of the conclusions reached or the opinions expressed.

Contents

Page

DIRECTOR'S STATEMENT xi

AUTHOR'S PREFACE xiii

Chapter

1. INTRODUCTION 1
   Purpose and Scope of This Study, 2

2. EXTRACTIVE OPERATIONS 6
   General Characteristics, 6
   Extractive Functions, 11
     Prospecting, 13
     Acquisition, 14
     Exploration, 15
     Development, 15
     Production, 17
   Classification of Mineral Reserves, 20
   *Joint Operations and Other Special Contractual
     Arrangements,* 20
     *Joint Exploration, Development, or Operating
       Arrangements,* 20
     Other Special Contractual Arrangements, 21

3. BASIC ACCOUNTING CONCEPTS AND PRINCIPLES ESPECIALLY
   APPLICABLE TO EXTRACTIVE OPERATIONS 22
   Basic Accounting Concepts and Principles, 23
   Cost Basis for Financial Statements, 24
   Realization Convention, 25
   Matching Process, 29
   Conservatism, 31
   Accounting for Income Taxes, 32
   Disclosure, 33
   Reporting Unit, 35
   Summary, 36

v

Chapter	Page
4. THE CAPITAL/EXPENSE DECISION 37	

    Survey of Present Practices, 38
        Accounting for Prospecting Costs, 38
            Geological and Geophysical Costs, 39
            Options to Acquire Mineral Rights, 41
            Summary of Practices, 41
        Accounting for Acquisition Costs, 42
        Accounting for Exploration Costs, 45
        Accounting for Development Costs, 49
            Petroleum Industry, 49
            Other Extractive Industries, 51
            Survey of Annual Reports, 52
            Summary of Accounting Practices, 53
        Accounting for Production Costs, 53
    Recommended Accounting Practices, 57
        Selection of a Cost Center, 57
            Mineral Deposit Recommended as the
              Appropriate Cost Center, 58
              Mineral deposit as a cost center, 58
              Cost centers based on acquisition units, 59
              Cost centers based on organization units, 60
        Allowing the Medium or the Nature of an
            Expenditure to Affect the Capital/Expense
            Decision, 65
        Transactions Occurring During the Prospecting
            and Acquisition Phases, 66
        Accounting for Transactions During the Period
            of Identification and Development of Mineral
            Reserves, 69
        Accounting for Hydrocarbons Purchased for
            Injection, 73
        Mine Restoration Costs, 74
        Summary of Recommendations Regarding the
            Capital/Expense Decision, 75

5. DISPOSITION OF CAPITALIZED COSTS 76	

    Survey of Present Practices, 76
        Accounting for the Disposition of Undeveloped
            Property Costs, 77
        Accounting for the Disposition of Producing
            Property and Equipment Costs, 79
        Effect of the Cost Center and Mineral Reserve
            Base on the Disposition of Capitalized Costs, 80
            Cost Center, 82
            Mineral Reserve Base, 83
        Summary of Present Practices, 84
    Recommended Accounting Practices, 86

Chapter	Page

Accounting for That Portion of Deferred Acquisition Costs Representing Prepaid Exploration Cost, 86
Accounting for the Disposition of Capitalized Costs Associated with Minerals-in-Place, 88
Definition of Total Reserve Quantity Benefited, 89
Allocation of Total Cost to Joint-Product Minerals, 90
Selection of Appropriate Stage in Extractive Operations to Measure Exhaustion of Capitalized Costs, 92
Depletion of Nonferrous Metal Mines, 92

6. ACCOUNTING FOR REVENUE, SPECIAL CONVEYANCES, AND JOINT OPERATIONS 94

Survey of Present Practices, 94
  Production Payments, 94
  ABC Transactions, 96
  Conveyances of Fractional Interests in Undeveloped Mineral Properties, 100
  Joint Operations, 102
Recommended Accounting Practices, 102
  Production Payments, 102
    Timing of Revenue, 104
    Classification of Deferred Proceeds, 105
  Sales Subject to Contingencies, 106
  Determining the Cost of Mineral Rights Acquired by Special Conveyances, 107
    Purchaser, 108
    Seller, 108
  Sales of Continuing Fractional Interests, 110

7. ACCOUNTING FOR FEDERAL INCOME TAXES 113

Percentage Depletion, 114
Geological and Geophysical Costs, 116
Costs of Successful Exploration—Other Than Oil and Gas, 118
IDC on Successful Wells in the Petroleum Industry, 118
Development Expenditures During the Production Stage of Mines, 122
Future Lifting Costs of Production to Satisfy a Retained Mineral Interest Payment, 123
Sale of Carved-Out Production Payment, 124
Amortization of Cost of Undeveloped Properties, 127
Revenue from Take-or-Pay Contracts and Gas Contract Price Increases Subject to Approval, 128
Summary and Conclusions, 128
Footnote to Chapter 7, 129

Chapter *Page*

8. PRESENTATION OF FINANCIAL STATEMENTS
 AND DISCLOSURE OF SUPPLEMENTARY INFORMATION
 IN FINANCIAL REPORTS 131

    *Description of Major Accounting Policies
 and Practices, 133*
       Recommended Practice, 133
       Present Practices Regarding Description of
         Major Accounting Policies and Practices, 134
     *Disclosure of Mineral Reserves and Operating
 Activities, 136*
       Recommended Practice, 136
       Present Practices Regarding Disclosure of
         Mineral Reserves and Operating Activities, 141
     Classification of Financial Accounts, 143
       Recommended Practice, 143
       Present Practice Regarding Classification of
         Financial Accounts, 145
     *Presentation of Total Capital Program
 Expenditures, 147*

9. SUMMARY 149

    Considerations Underlying Recommendations, 149
     The Capital/Expense Decision, 150
     Disposition of Capitalized Costs, 151
     Accounting for Revenue, Special Conveyances,
       and Joint Operations, 152
     Accounting for Federal Income Taxes, 153
     Recommended Presentation and Disclosure
       Practices, 153

COMMENTS BY MEMBERS OF PROJECT
ADVISORY COMMITTEE 155

    Comments of Gordon T. Bethune, 155
     Comments of R. Hersel Hughes,
       Richard M. McGowen, and
       Charles W. Plum, 155

Appendix

A. MINERAL PRODUCTION IN THE UNITED STATES,
 1963-1966 159

B. EXCERPTS FROM "DEPLETION ALLOWANCES FOR
 MINERAL PRODUCTION REPORTED ON U. S. TAX
 RETURNS". 164

Appendix	Page
C. LIST OF 265 COMPANIES WHOSE 1964 ANNUAL REPORTS WERE REVIEWED FOR DISCLOSURE PRACTICES	173
D. GLOSSARY	177
SELECTED BIBLIOGRAPHY	181

Director's Statement

This study demonstrates that discovering and extracting irreplaceable natural resources create accounting problems not encountered in other industries. The problems of accounting for extractive industries are also numerous and diverse. The importance of the study, however, is not in the differences between the various extractive industries and between the extractive and other industries that Robert E. Field finds, but in the similarities.

Mr. Field's emphasis on the basic similarities of various extractive industries enables him to analyze their accounting problems as a group rather than to treat each industry separately. The proposed solutions apply to all extractive industries.

The study also shows that the accounting problems of the extractive industries are not so unique that they must be solved with entirely new accounting. That is, the nature of the problems, such as matching costs with revenue and choosing cost centers to relate costs and benefits, is much the same as that in manufacturing operations. The study thus principally concerns applying some accepted fundamental accounting ideas to particular types of operations and products which are unique to extractive industries.

Applying accepted concepts to special types of situations often requires looking at them in unaccustomed ways. Accountants usually discuss depletable assets in the same terms as depreciable assets, and this connection tends to affect the way a problem is seen and solved. This study treats natural resources as similar to inventories rather than to plant and equipment. That insight is important to the reasoning in the study because matching inventory costs with revenue in present accounting differs in important respects from matching plant and equipment costs with revenue. For example, inventory accounting is characterized by an attempt to trace cause and effect—the costs of purchase and production and the revenue from sale of product—to a significant degree, but depreciation accounting is characterized only by an attempt to match costs with revenue in a systematic and rational way.

I wish to express my appreciation to Mr. Field and to the firm of which he is partner, Price Waterhouse & Co., for making this contribution to the accounting research program of the American Institute of Certified Public Accountants.

I also wish to express my appreciation to members of the project advisory committee for valuable assistance and for reviewing several drafts of the study. All present members of the committee favored publication of the study, and four members have contributed comments which are published following the study (pages 155 to 157). Approval of publication by a committee member or restriction of his comments to specific parts or aspects of the study should not be interpreted as his concurrence with the contents, conclusions, or recommendations of the study.

The Accounting Principles Board will consider this study and hopes that interested individuals and groups will read the study carefully and submit comments on it. The Board will review the comments received. Comments submitted will be most useful to the Board if they cover not only the conclusions but also the analysis, premises, and arguments and include supporting reasoning.

New York, N. Y., November 1969   REED K. STOREY
Director of Accounting Research

Author's Preface

This is the first accounting research study to analyze and recommend financial reporting practices of a group of related industries with common operating objectives and characteristics. My experience leads me to believe that the industry approach to accounting research is sound. The fact that relatively few divergent opinions were expressed by members of the project advisory committee selected from several of the extractive industries seems to support the existence of a common thread of logic to be expressed in financial reporting of extractive operations, even though methods of operation and the language of the several extractive industries differ.

An impediment to the study was the absence of a comprehensive, authoritative pronouncement on the basic concepts and principles of accounting applicable to the financial statements of all profit-making organizations. The Accounting Principles Board is now preparing and hopefully will soon issue an authoritative Statement on the basic concepts and accounting principles underlying financial statements of business enterprises which will remedy this condition.

This study could not have been completed without the assistance of many people who provided technical knowledge of specific extractive industries and who reviewed and commented on the proposed material. Unfortunately, the list of those persons who contributed is too long to enumerate in its entirety, but I want to express my gratitude to all who participated with so much genuine interest and enthusiasm and willingness to help. In particular, I wish to acknowledge the valuable contributions made to this study by Reed K. Storey, Director of Accounting Research of the American Institute of Certified Public Accountants, his associates, Thomas W. McRae, Paul H. Rosenfield, and Rudolph W. Schattke, and the members of the project advisory committee. The present members of the project advisory committee are: Herman W. Bevis, *Chairman*, Gordon T. Bethune, John F. Frawley, R. Hersel Hughes, Edward W. Kay, Richard M. McGowen, Charles W. Plum, and Glenn A. Welsch. Others who served as committee members are: Robert W. Boyd, Thomas N. Herreid, Wallace Macgregor, Cecil E. Munn, and Max S. Simpson. I also wish to acknowledge the assistance of Professor Horace R. Brock of North Texas State University and of Harold T. Dokupil, Albert C. Henry, and Gary Scott Schieneman of the staff of Price Waterhouse & Co.

Credit for major contribution is due the American Petroleum Institute for its "Report of Certain Petroleum Industry Accounting Practices—1965," and for its *ad hoc* liaison committee formed to review this project. The API report demonstrates what can be done by an industry, on its own initiative, to bring together for consideration and evaluation the major accounting practices underlying financial reports.

Finally, I want to pay tribute to Paul Grady, whose wisdom and counsel have been an inspiration to me for many years and who, while serving as Director of Accounting Research for the Institute, asked me to undertake this study.

New York, N. Y., November 1969   ROBERT E. FIELD

1

Introduction

The production of minerals adds some $23 billion a year (1966[1]) to gross national product and commands a prominent role in capital formation and investment. The magnitude of expenditures in extractive operations, the romantic appeal of the search for rare minerals, and the prospect of high return on investment have established a prominent place for the extractive industries among investment media.

Extractive operations contain many unusual features which, when coupled with widespread appeal to investors, make the extractive industries particularly well adapted to industry-wide analysis of operations and recommendations for common financial reporting practices. The complexities of operations multiply the opportunities for differences in opinion on what constitutes the best reporting. Without guidance, the possibility of confusing investors by the use of differing practices is relatively greater than in most other industries.

Most investors have little firsthand knowledge of corporate operations and must depend on the management to provide appropriate information. The basic needs of the investor are met primarily by annual reports to stockholders, including statistical and financial data, supplemented occasionally by a prospectus for the sale or exchange of securities. As the principal means of communication from management to investor concerning the financial status and progress of the company, these reports should be not only timely but also complete and understandable.

Management plays a significant role in producing full and fair disclosure in financial reports. Managers have firsthand knowledge of present operations, past experience, and future probabilities which

---

[1] United States Department of the Interior, Bureau of Mines, *Minerals Yearbook 1966*, Volume I-II, 1967, p. 105.

constitute the basis for the representations contained in the financial statements. Management quite properly has the primary responsibility for selection of accounting practices and presentation of financial statements. However, the viewpoints of various management groups are likely to differ, and complete freedom of choice in selecting accounting practices could lead to a variety of reported results among companies in comparable operating circumstances. This would detract from the usefulness of financial reports in comparing the results of operations of different companies in the same industry.

Orientation of accounting practice to common concepts will contribute to comparable financial statements. So will agreement to use the same accounting practice in comparable operating circumstances where they can be identified. Surface indications of similarity, however, do not always reflect comparable operating circumstances. Recommended accounting concepts and practices can provide guidelines to management; they cannot provide categorical, precise rules for reporting transactions without consideration of individual circumstances.

2 Purpose and Scope of This Study

The purpose of this research study is to evaluate financial reporting practices in the extractive industries by considering the distinctive elements of extractive operations, the investor's need for information, and the applicable concepts of general accounting theory and to select and recommend appropriate accounting and reporting practices. The recommendations are intended to lead to improvement of financial reporting to investors in the extractive industries by encouraging the adoption of better methods of reporting and the narrowing of alternative accounting practices to those that reflect differences in operating circumstances.

This study encompasses financial reporting in the extractive industries, identified as:

1. Petroleum and natural gas
2. Coal
3. Metals
4. Nonmetallic minerals.[2]

---

[2] Conceivably, timber might be included among the extractive industries. This was considered but rejected because of the regenerating nature of the resource.

Chapter 2 describes extractive operations in each of five functions: prospecting, acquisition, exploration, development, and production. It also contains discussions of the methods of classifying mineral reserves and of contractual arrangements which are prevalent in the industry. Chapter 3 sets forth the basic concepts and accounting principles applicable to these operations. Accounting and reporting practices are described in Chapters 4 to 8, and recommendations are made for appropriate application of the basic concepts and principles. A summary of the study is presented in Chapter 9.

The following are appended:

1. Appendix A, a tabulation of mineral production in the United States 1963-1966.

2. Appendix B, excerpts from a U. S. Treasury Department publication describing computation of the depletion allowance and explaining other terms having special tax significance.

3. Appendix C, a list of 265 companies whose 1964 annual reports were reviewed for disclosure practices.

4. Appendix D, a glossary.

Finally, a bibliography is provided for background in both operations and accounting practices. One listed source, *Economics of the Mineral Industries*, is an especially comprehensive description of extractive operations. A similarly comprehensive analysis of the common financial reporting problems inherent in finding and producing economically recoverable minerals does not appear to be available. The published literature on accounting and financial reporting problems in the extractive industries is oriented to individual industries with an emphasis on oil and gas and hard-rock metal mining. The preponderance of material on petroleum accounting and reporting practices is attributable to several factors. In contrast to other extractive industries, the petroleum industry involves substantially greater investment in acquisition and development costs prior to production of a mineral reserve and relatively little production cost. Companies in other extractive industries incur development and production costs in successive stages as production advances, and these costs represent the major part of expenditures, whereas acquisition costs are relatively less important. The greater variety and magnitude of costs incurred prior to production and sale of minerals in the petroleum industry multiply the number of difficult decisions necessary in arriving at the most reasonable basis for relating expenditures to particular operating periods.

In addition, the very large commitments of venture capital required in petroleum operations before production is obtained, or even is known to be obtainable, encourage many complicated legal arrangements to spread the greater risk or to obtain maximum allowable tax benefits. Each of these arrangements presents accounting problems.

Finally, the petroleum and natural gas industry is by far the most significant source of mineral production in the United States. The value of production in this industry in 1966, $12.5 billion, was 54% of the $23 billion total value of mineral production in that year. Of the other minerals, only coal output amounted to as much as 10% of total mineral production. The summary in Table 1, opposite, indicates the relative output by major industry classification; details are given in Appendix A.

The published material on extractive industries other than petroleum has been supplemented by use of reports on accounting practices in each industry obtained as background for *Accounting Research Study No. 7*, "Inventory of Generally Accepted Accounting Principles for Business Enterprises," by Paul Grady, published in 1965. Each report was prepared by a firm of independent accountants especially experienced in the particular industry. The reports describe industry accounting practices and identify major and minor usages but do not indicate the relative number of companies using each alternative practice.

The material already available was further supplemented by inquiry of industry officials. Representatives of some 20 companies producing cement (limestone), phosphate, sulfur, stone, gravel, and sand participated in discussions of the financial reporting problems in those industries.

The extent of disclosure of accounting and operational data discussed in Chapter 8 of this study is based on a review of the 1964 annual reports of 265 extractive industries companies. Some observations on accounting practices are available as a by-product of that review. However, only a small minority of companies made positive disclosure of most of the accounting practices followed. Although many of the practices followed could be inferred from account descriptions and footnotes, the overall results of the review were not definitive enough to support general conclusions about accounting practices. Information from the review of annual reports, when used

TABLE 1

Mineral Production — United States

| | 1966 Output ||
Industry Classification	Value (Thousands)	Percent of Total
Mineral fuels:		
Petroleum, natural gas and natural gas liquids	$12,497,120	54.6
Coal	2,521,956	11.0
Other	88,924	.4
Total Mineral Fuels	15,108,000	66.0
Nonmetals (except fuels):		
Cement and lime	1,466,841	6.4
Stone	1,260,715	5.5
Sand and gravel	984,982	4.3
Other	1,464,462	6.4
Total Nonmetals	5,177,000	22.6
Metals:		
Copper	1,033,850	4.5
Iron ore	854,134	3.7
Other	733,016	3.2
Total Metals	2,621,000	11.4
Grand Total Mineral Production	$22,906,000	100.0

in connection with the discussion of current practice, should be regarded as illustrative of the statements of general practice based on the authorities cited rather than as conclusive evidence of general practice.

2

Extractive Operations

General Characteristics

The extractive industries are characterized by the exposure of invested capital to a relatively high degree of risk over an extended period of time. Risk is inherent in the search for natural resource deposits because there is no assurance that they will be found or, if found, that they will be of commercial quantity and grade. The risk is usually compounded by a relatively long production period during which there may be substantial changes in estimated volume and value of mineral deposits because of changes in extraction technologies, changes in market demand, or shortcomings of the techniques for measuring reserve quantities.

The degree of risk varies among the extractive industries. Although all mineral deposits are limited to the quantities and locations fixed by natural processes, these limits in some instances are so broad as to be largely academic (in terms of present needs) and in other instances so narrow as to be highly critical. Thus, sand and gravel may be found in ample supply in almost all localities, whereas the presence of oil and precious metals in commercial quantities is conjectural in any area.

For most minerals, the natural limits on reserves are not as significant as the economic limits: exploitable reserves (in terms of present economic conditions) are substantially less than theoretical reserves.[1]

---

[1] A specialist in the field, Elmer W. Pehrson, discusses this point in "Minerals in National and International Affairs." *Economics of the Mineral Industries*, Edward H. Robie, editor, Second Edition, 1964, Chapter 11, pp. 525-528.

Table 1, page 8, compares exploitable and theoretical reserves for selected minerals.

The relative degree of exploratory effort tends to vary inversely with years of supply of exploitable reserves. For example, few companies are searching for coal at the present time; but substantial amounts are being spent in searching for oil, gas, and many metals. Consequently, the exposure of capital to the risk of nonproductive exploratory efforts is greater in these last three industries.

About one out of nine new-field wildcat exploratory petroleum wells results in a discovery, but only one in about thirty new-field wildcats results in discovery of a commercially profitable field (defined as one having more than one million barrels of oil reserves or six billion cubic feet of gas reserves). The average cost of drilling a well is about $55,000 but individual well costs range far from this average; for example, the average cost of wells over 15,000 feet deep is $715,000.[2] Moreover, these amounts exclude predrilling costs which may be substantial. *Economics of the Mineral Industries*[3] reports that the average cost for a wildcat well, including exploration expenses necessary to locate it, is approximately $160,000 and that it costs about $5,000,000 to find a commercial oil or gas field.

The search for metals is similarly costly. Reported Canadian experience indicates that the typical cost of finding a mine is $7,500,000, including geological and geophysical studies and exploratory drilling.[4] It is interesting to note that only 1.54% of all metal mining companies in Ontario during the 50-year period, 1904 to 1953, were economically successful in the sense that they paid dividends.[5]

Even though finding costs may not be particularly large, substantial investments in development facilities and equipment usually are required. These investments are recoverable from sales of future production which may or may not prove to be as much as originally estimated. Relatively long periods of time are required to exploit mineral deposits. Many changes can occur in market demand, foreign imports, government controls, and so forth, with unpredictable effects upon the market

---

[2] American Petroleum Institute, *Petroleum Facts and Figures*, 1967, p. 29.

[3] John R. Crandall, J. W. Glanville, and L. Cookenboo, "Cost of Acquiring and Operating Mineral Properties—Petroleum and Natural Gas," Edward H. Robie, editor, Second Edition, 1964, Chapter 5, Part 2, p. 232.

[4] J. D. Bateman, "Exploration Program for Small Mining Companies," *Mining Congress Journal*, December 1963, p. 45.

[5] V. C. Wansbrough, "Financing Mining Ventures—A Canadian View," *Mining Congress Journal*, November 1963, p. 36.

TABLE 1

Quantitative Comparisons of Theoretical Resources and Exploitable Reserves in the Lithosphere with 1962 World Production, for Selected Minerals[1]

	Theoretical Availability to Attainable Depths[2]		Estimated Exploitable Reserve,[3] Billion (10⁹) Metric Tons	Ratio Exploitable to Theoretical, One to:	1962 World Production,[4] Metric Tons	Years of Supply of Exploitable Reserve[5]
	Average Content, Percent	Total Resources, Billion (10⁹) Metric Tons				
Energy Minerals						
Coal	n.a.	15,000	4700.	3	2,678,000,000	1755
Petroleum	n.a.	700	50.	14	1,215,000,000	41
Natural Gas	n.a.	190	18.	11	500,000,000	36
Common Metals						
Aluminum	8.13	100,812,000	2.	50,406,000	5,040,000	397
Iron	5.0	62,000,000	131.	473,000	282,000,000	464
Manganese	0.1	1,240,000	0.5	2,480,000	6,670,000	75
Chromium	0.02	248,000	0.7	354,000	1,310,000	535
Zinc	0.0132	164,000	0.25	656,000	3,515,000	71
Nickel	0.008	99,000	0.05	1,980,000	362,000	138
Copper	0.007	87,000	0.25	348,000	4,600,000	54
Tin	0.004	50,000	0.007	7,143,000	193,000	36
Lead	0.0016	19,800	0.15	132,000	2,510,000	60
Gold	0.0000001	1.24	0.00003	41,000	1,550	20
Space-Age Metals						
Titanium	0.44	5,456,000	0.15	36,370,000	1,000,000	150
Zirconium	0.022	273,000	0.02	13,650,000	105,000	190
Tungsten	0.005	62,000	0.001	62,000,000	33,000	30
Columbium	0.0024	29,800	0.0125	2,380,000	2,200	5700
Cobalt	0.0023	28,500	0.003	9,500,000	18,000	165
Beryllium	0.0006	7,400	n.a.	n.a.	300	n.a.
Uranium	0.0004	5,000	0.001	5,000,000	40,000	25
Molybdenum	0.0003	3,700	0.004	925,000	34,100	115
Fertilizer Elements						
Potassium	2.59	32,116,000	43.	747,000	8,050,000	5350
Phosphorus	0.118	1,463,000	7.	209,000	6,550,000	1070
Sulphur	0.052	645,000	n.a.	n.a.	20,445,000	n.a.

[1] After a study by Ferdinand Friedensburg, "The Future Supply of Metals," *Zeitschrift fur Erzbergbau und Metallhuttenwesen*, Dec. 1957, pp. 573–576.

n.a. indicates authoritative data or satisfactory basis for estimation are unavailable.

[2] Geochemical data chiefly from Geochemistry: Rankama, Kalervo, and Sahama, Th.G.; Univ. of Chicago Press, 1950. Quantitative data except for energy minerals represent content of a 3000-meter crust of the lithosphere; estimated gross weight 1,240 × 10¹⁵ metric tons. Petroleum and natural gas resources currently are worked to depths approximating 7,500 meters. Coal resources generally are limited to a depth of 1000 meters. Hard-rock mining is conducted to depths of 3000 meters. Resource data for petroleum and natural gas from Weeks, Lewis G.: Fuel Reserves of the Future; *Bul. Amer. Assoc. Petroleum Geologists*, vol. 42, No. 2, pp. 431–441, Feb. 1958, and Hubbert, M. King: Energy Resources, A Report to the Committee on Natural Resources, National Academy of Sciences—National Research Council, Publication 1000-D, Washington D.C., 1962.

[3] *Source:* Chiefly compilations of the United States Geological Survey, the Federal Bureau of Mines, and Resources for the Future, Inc., supplemented by a few estimates by author for Sino-Soviet bloc areas.

[4] *Source:* Chiefly U.S. Bureau of Mines.

[5] At 1962 rate of production. The figure shown for coal does not allow for losses in mining which may exceed 50 percent in the United States; elsewhere losses seldom exceed 15 percent.

Source: *Economics of the Mineral Industries,* Edward H. Robie, editor, Second Edition, 1964, Chapter 11, p. 526.

value of remaining minerals. Technological changes may increase or decrease the quantities of commercially exploitable minerals in any one industry, depending on whether the changes benefit that industry or a competitive one. Both the coal and iron ore industries provide illustrations of the importance of outside events on economic feasibility of mineral recovery.

Until recently, the coal industry was depressed. Markets fell off during the 1930's because of competition from oil, and the home-heating market almost disappeared in the 1940's under the added competition from natural gas. Yet the coal industry has made a comeback, principally for electric generation, in large part because of technological innovations such as unit trains and mine-mouth generating plants, as well as increased mechanization of mining methods.

Similarly, in the iron ore industry, the Mesabi range, depleted of its rich direct-shipment ores, had at one time become essentially dormant. Production of Mesabi iron ore is now being revived by a combination of technological change, including the beneficiation of taconite, and improved local tax climate.

The transitory nature of reserve estimates is illustrated in the petroleum industry. For years additions to reserves through revisions of previous estimates and extensions to known fields have far exceeded additions to reserves through discoveries of new fields and new pools in old fields. Table 2, page 10, shows reserves and changes in reserves by sources for the years 1958 to 1966. The revisions and extensions in column 1 of that table reflect not only more extensive knowledge of the fields resulting from progressive development over several years, but also the advent of new production methods and changes in market conditions which increase the quantity of commercially recoverable reserves.

In some situations, the future is so uncertain that complete definition of mineral deposits is not attempted; reserves are proved only to the extent necessary to indicate whether further development is warranted. The following excerpt from the text of the 1964 annual report of Copper Range Company illustrates some of the problems in estimating reserves:

> *Ore Reserves*
>
> No plan for expansion can be undertaken until the presence of adequate reserves of ore has been determined. Several years of careful geological studies, based upon the information obtained from diamond drilling, have given us a more profound knowledge

TABLE 2
U. S. RESERVES OF LIQUID HYDROCARBONS, 1958-1966

(Thousands of Barrels)

Year	Revisions	Extensions	Reserves Discovered in New Fields	Reserves Discovered in New Pools in Old Fields	Production During Year	Proved Reserves at End of Year	Net Change	Indicated Additional Reserves from Known Reservoirs
CRUDE OIL
1966	1,839,307	814,249	160,384	150,038	2,864,242	31,452,127	99,736	7,594,019
1965	1,783,231	792,901	237,335	234,612	2,686,198	31,352,391	361,881	....
1964	899,292	1,419,182	126,682	219,611	2,644,247	30,990,510	20,520	....
1963	966,051	858,168	96,732	253,159	2,593,343	30,969,990	−419,233	....
1962	759,053	1,041,257	92,488	288,098	2,550,178	31,389,223	−369,282	....
1961	1,087,092	1,209,101	107,423	253,951	2,512,273	31,758,505	145,294	....
1960	787,934	1,323,538	141,296	112,560	2,471,464	31,613,211	−106,136	....
1959	1,518,678	1,778,705	165,695	203,667	2,483,315	31,719,347	1,183,430	....
1958	954,605	1,338,908	151,210	163,519	2,372,730	30,535,917	235,512	....
NATURAL GAS LIQUIDS
1966	634,233	131,583	53,378	74,922	588,684	8,328,966	305,432	....
1965			110,707		555,410	8,023,534	276,902	....
1964	721,605		151,042		536,090	7,746,632	72,654	....
1963	457,702		177,937		515,659	7,673,978	362,461	....
1962	700,183		151,979		470,128	7,311,517	262,421	....
	580,570							
1961	590,537		104,149		461,649	7,049,096	233,037	....
1960	603,621		121,509		431,379	6,816,059	293,751	....
1959	593,905		109,539		385,154	6,522,308	318,290	....
1958	749,956		108,250		341,548	6,204,018	516,658	....
TOTAL LIQUID HYDROCARBONS
1966	2,473,540	945,832	213,762	224,960	3,452,926	39,781,093	405,168	7,594,019
1965	3,297,737		582,654		3,241,608	39,375,925	638,783	....
1964	2,776,176		497,335		3,180,337	38,737,142	93,174	....
1963	2,524,402		527,828		3,109,002	38,643,968	−56,772	....
1962	2,380,880		532,565		3,020,306	38,700,740	−106,861	....
1961	2,886,730		465,523		2,973,922	38,807,601	378,331	....
1960	2,715,093		375,365		2,902,843	38,429,270	187,615	....
1959	3,891,288		478,901		2,868,469	38,241,655	1,501,720	....
1958	3,043,469		422,979		2,714,278	36,739,935	752,170	....

Source: American Petroleum Institute, *Petroleum Facts and Figures*, 1967, p. 57.

of the size, extent and characteristics of the White Pine orebody. Although we have by no means drilled out or delineated all of our potential ore reserves, their size is now known to be more than double what we knew about four years ago. In each of these four years we carried on a development drilling program which has added an increment to the reserves each year. Holes drilled during the 1964 season alone indicated no less than 60 million additional tons of the grade and kind of ore we are mining today. This is more than has been mined since White Pine started ten years ago! Thus, we know today that the White Pine ore reserve is larger, in proportion to its present productive capacity, than any copper mine in the U.S.—and probably the world. This reserve, in all likelihood, contains as much as 10 per cent of the total U.S. copper reserves (in contained copper—not tons of ore). We have so much ore of the present grade ahead of us that it is not realistic to continue our drilling program until we have firmly established the economics of mining it under the new method.

We have little basis for estimating how much more is contained in lands which we control. We do not like to give a tonnage figure for ore reserves, as the actual ore is a function of price and cost of extraction. The higher the price, the lower grade ore we can mine. For instance, the increase of three cents in the price this year theoretically would add some 120 million tons to the known reserves on which the above statements were predicated. It is safe to say that we have ore reserves to last us at the present rate of extraction for nearly one hundred years and therefore are safe in planning a major expansion of production.

Extractive Functions

In this study, the process of finding and recovering minerals is described in terms of five operational phases or functions: (1) prospecting, (2) acquisition, (3) exploration, (4) development, and (5) production. In practice the phases may overlap; for example, prospecting is not always distinguished from exploration.

The distinction among these five phases is not consistent among the four industries under study nor even among companies within each of the industries. Clear-cut distinctions are quite rare in the metals and nonmetallic minerals industries where exploration, development, and production phases of operations frequently merge.

In a continuing survey conducted jointly by the American Petroleum Institute, the Independent Petroleum Association of America, and the Mid-Continent Oil & Gas Association, estimated expenditures for finding, developing, and producing oil and gas in the United States for the years 1962 to 1966 are classified as shown in Table 3 on page 12.

TABLE 3

Estimated Expenditures for Finding, Developing, and Producing Oil and Gas in the United States, 1962-1966

Expenditures	1962	1963	1964	1965	1966
		— Millions —			
Exploration:					
Dry Hole Costs	$ 847	$ 790	$ 854	$ 849	$ 832
Lease Acquisition	815	376	570	438	577
Lease Rentals	197	193	177	166	180
Geological & Geophysical	299	300	336	355	378
Land, Leasing, & Scouting Expenses	108	117	100	102	70
Other	58	69	72	61	128
Total	$2,324	$1,845	$2,109	$1,971	$2,165
Development:					
Drilling & Equipping Producing Wells	$1,729	$1,512	$1,574	$1,553	$1,528
Equipping Leases	537	527	619	580	878
Total	$2,266	$2,039	$2,193	$2,133	$2,406
Production:					
Producing Costs	$1,535	$1,581	$1,613	$1,685	$1,895
Production Taxes	354	373	393	400	430
Ad Valorem Taxes	202	198	204	212	212
Total	$2,091	$2,152	$2,210	$2,297	$2,537
Overhead:					
Exploration	$ 213	$ 200	$ 215	$ 207	$ 195
Development & Production	478	470	461	487	478
Total	$ 691	$ 670	$ 676	$ 694	$ 673
Total Expenditures:*	$7,372	$6,706	$7,188	$7,095	$7,781

* Exclusive of federal, state, and local income taxes; payments of interest; payments for the retirement of debt; and payments to owners as return on investment.

Source: *Joint Association Survey* (Section 2), "Estimated Expenditures & Receipts of U.S. Oil and Gas Producing Industry," 1966.

Although similarly quantified and classified composite data are not available for other extractive industries, the following observations regarding relative significance of expenditures in the various phases of operation can be drawn from the literature.

Very little prospecting for new reserves is being done in the coal industry. Known reserves are sufficient to satisfy expected demand for more than 1,700 years and expenditures are directed mainly to development and production.

Prospecting and exploration for metals are still significant functions. Development expenditures in this industry are not completely distinguishable from either exploration or production costs. All three activities are frequently carried on at the same time. In deep mines the shafts and drifts required for exploration frequently provide a means of access for development of ore bodies.

It is not easy to generalize about the nonmetallic minerals industry. Some minerals, such as limestone, sand, and gravel, are relatively common, and discovery requires little prospecting expenditure. Exploration, which consists principally of defining limits of known mineral deposits, and development and production tend to go hand in hand. Many of the other nonmetallic minerals, however, are rare and substantial discovery costs are involved.

In summary, the extractive processes of prospecting, acquisition, exploration, development, and production are not equally identifiable or measurable among the industries being studied. They are, however, common processes which present common financial reporting problems. Each process involves substantial expenditure in one industry or another, although not in the same order of magnitude.

Prospecting. This study uses the term "prospecting" (not always distinguished from "exploration" in common usage) to describe the search for geological information leading to acquisition of exploration rights in areas of further interest. Prospecting ranges from general observation of industry activity and broad surveillance to extensive and costly detailed physical tests in particular geographical areas. The degree of prospecting effort varies from industry to industry in accordance with the adequacy of known resources to meet expected future demands, but it is to some degree at least a continuing activity essential to any extractive enterprise. The intent is to narrow the search for minerals to areas of greater promise by obtaining evidence of structures which experience indicates may contain minerals. Prospecting is a necessary preliminary to acquisition and exploration by which the presence of minerals is either proved or disproved.

Prospecting methods are commonly grouped under the term "geological and geophysical studies." These processes consist of seeking surface or subterranean indications of earth structures or formations of a type which experience has shown indicates the possibility of mineral deposits. Although many of the important mines now producing were discovered by visual observation of surface outcroppings, and although some mineral deposits will undoubtedly continue to be found by this means, more sophisticated methods have been developed to locate the less obvious deposits in very deep structures.

Prospecting usually begins by obtaining or preparing and reviewing topographical and geological maps covering a particular area of interest. Aerial photography is frequently used. This initial process may reveal the presence of surface formations favorable to mineral deposits, and thus pinpoint areas for more intensive geophysical surveys.

The geophysicist takes advantage of the fact that natural properties of minerals indicate the presence of something different in the earth's structure—an "anomaly" in mining parlance. Changes in magnetic force or gravity, distinctive patterns of conductivity in response to seismic waves or electric currents, or chemical content of soils (determined by geochemistry) may indicate the possibility of mineral deposits. Magnetometers, gravimeters, and seismographs are examples of instruments used in these activities.

The elements of cost during this phase of operations include: options to lease or buy property; rights of access to lands for geophysical work; and salaries, equipment, and supplies for scouts, geologists, and geophysical crews. Although some geological and geophysical work is done by a company's own force, the major part is usually done by outside contractors who are specialists in the field.

Acquisition. The right to explore a prospect and to recover any minerals discovered is obtained by lease or purchase of land and mineral rights or of mineral rights alone. Leasing of mineral rights alone is the most common form of acquisition in the petroleum industry; purchase of mineral rights or of land and mineral rights is more common in other industries. The usual lease calls for a bonus upon signing, sometimes very substantial as in the case of offshore petroleum operations, and a royalty on any minerals produced. Minimum advance royalties, usually recoverable from future production, may be required. Leases usually require the lessee to carry out specified work within certain periods of time or to make additional payments (delay rentals) if the work is delayed.

Mineral rights may be purchased in fee or acquired by lease either before or after the exploration process. Ordinarily purchase options or acreage selection options are taken early in the prospecting stage.

Other acquisition costs include lease brokers' commissions, abstract and recording fees, legal fees, and title search fees. Costs to retain exploration and property rights after acquisition but before production (commonly called "carrying costs") include legal costs for title defense and *ad valorem* taxes on unmined reserves, as well as the minimum royalties and delay rentals mentioned above.

Exploration. Exploration in its early stages may use some of the same geophysical techniques as prospecting. Although these functions together might be considered one process—the finding of minerals—they are distinguishable by objectives: prospecting seeks an area of probable mineralization; exploration probes that area for specific deposits.

A favorable prospect can be proved only by some means of physical access to the expected mineral body—by activities such as drilling, tunneling, and removal of overburden. Discovery, if successful, is followed by extension of these efforts to define the prospect further and to determine the likelihood of its being commercially productive.

Exploration methods include drilling of wells or cores, underground shafts, drifts, and crosscuts and, in some cases, the removal of overburden. Costs comprise labor, administrative overhead, depreciation of drilling and mining equipment, mining supplies, and some access or support facilities such as housing for crews in remote areas. Exploration may be done by a company's own force or by independent companies under contract. Exploratory efforts of other persons in the petroleum fields are often aided by dry-hole or bottom-hole contributions for which the donor receives drilling knowledge but no economic interest in production.

Exploratory costs are a larger part of the total mining effort in the petroleum and metals industries than in the coal and nonmetallic minerals industries such as sand, gravel, and stone. However, they may be substantial in other nonmetallic minerals industries in which the minerals are in short supply or are deposited in deep beds.

Development. Development of a mineral discovery for commercial production requires the construction of access and mineral-handling facilities. The main mineral body must be opened to further mining by drilling, removing overburden, sinking shafts, or driving tunnels. Roads, dikes, primary cleaning or processing equipment, and field storage are required to move, store, and prepare minerals for shipment. Supporting facilities for housing and care of work force may be required, particularly in isolated locations.

Development work is usually carried out by contract, but it may also be performed by a company's own force. Most of these development expenditures are not recoverable in the event that mining is discontinued because they consist largely of labor and construction equipment costs, and also because of the impracticability of removing equipment.

A mine is said to be in the development phase prior to the time production on a commercial scale is obtained. Development expenditures, however, are made not only during the development phase but subsequently to extend production. A mine can be, and usually is, in commercial production before all reserves are developed. This condition is common in strip, quarry, or shaft mining where the entire mineral body is developed gradually as mining progresses. To some extent, development in successive stages as one of these mines is extended is a function of production since successive removals of ore must be made to uncover unmined reserves. But development in successive stages is also a matter of choice, for it avoids a substantial commitment of capital in access tunnels and shafts or in removing overburden before these improvements are required for production. Usually development of the mineral body proceeds a year or two in advance of production, with a somewhat longer period for open-pit mines.

Some development costs can be incurred only as mining progresses. For example, in hard-rock mines additional tracks, lighting, and ventilation must be provided as the working face recedes and roofs must usually be supported by timber, roof bolts, or pillars of minerals. Development work in reverse can occur when the mine is exhausted. Equipment is salvaged and pillars of minerals are removed during the withdrawal process.

Development in successive stages also pertains, but to a lesser extent, to deep mining of petroleum, gas, and nonmetallic minerals, such as sulfur or salt. Petroleum and gas reservoirs are developed rather rapidly in their entirety once production is decided on. Early definition of the limits and conditions of the reservoir facilitates an efficient plan of production to ensure maximum recovery; the speed and intensity of development are consistent with regulations of state conservation authorities relating to well-spacing and maximum rate of production.

To a considerable extent, the nature of expenditures and the types of facilities which result from development are not different from those classified as exploration. Development expenditures for wells, shafts, tunnels, and drifts are frequently extensions or augmentations of similar facilities that were provided during exploration. They become in turn equally useful for subsequent development and production.

The risks involved in development expenditures are considerably less than those which attend prospecting and exploration because a mineral deposit is now known to exist. Risks are not eliminated, however. Changes in market prices or competitive conditions and errors in original estimates of reserves can make recovery of development investment uneconomical. Furthermore, individual applications of development effort may be unsuccessful. For example, one out of every four petroleum development wells drilled in 1966 was unsuccessful, even though an accumulation of hydrocarbons had been proved to be present by exploratory drilling.[6] This ratio can be compared with a success ratio of one out of nine for new-field wildcat wells, and one out of 30 for commercially successful new-field wildcat wells.

Production. Production facilities include the tunnels, shafts, wells, equipment and other facilities constructed during the development process, and mining or processing equipment which may be either permanent or movable. Labor is a substantial part of production cost, especially in hard-rock mining, strip mining, and quarry operations.

Production methods vary, depending on the depth and width of the ore deposit and the manner in which it lies. Petroleum, natural gas, and deep minerals, such as sulfur, are ordinarily produced from wells. Some minor quantities of petroleum are obtained from kerogen in oil shale which is mined from the surface. Surface mining by quarry or pit is the more common method of producing most coal, metal, and nonmetallic mineral ores in bulk, but substantial quantities are taken also from underground mines. Mining methods frequently require blasting or mechanical digging that may result in quantities of broken ore in a pit or underground mine. These quantities may be substantial when techniques such as underground caving are used to break large blocks of ore away from surrounding rock. The production of petroleum and sulfur from deep wells results in no similar partially processed product in the mine, but temporary field storage above ground must be provided. Natural gas flows directly from underground reservoirs into

---

[6] American Petroleum Institute, *Petroleum Facts and Figures*, 1967, p. 13.

sales channels, sometimes passing through a processing plant for removal of heavy hydrocarbons.

According to the U. S. Bureau of Mines, surface mining contributed 94% of the metallic and nonmetallic ores and 95% of total material handled in 1966. Surface mining provided 83% of crude ore from metal mines and 96% of nonmetallic minerals. Further indication of the relative significance of surface and underground mining of particular metals and nonmetallic minerals is shown in Table 4, opposite. The production of coal from surface mines amounts to more than 30% of total coal mined.

Underground conditions create many operating problems which lead to higher production costs, or in some cases to abandonment of part or all of the access facilities. For example, the natural pressures in an oil reservoir will provide sufficient drive to produce, typically, only 20% to 30% of the oil in place; water flooding or gas injection to drive oil to the well, or other secondary recovery methods, are used to increase total recovery (but even under the most advanced recovery methods probably no more than 80% to 85% of the oil in the reservoir will be recovered). Also, producing wells in oil and gas fields frequently require workovers or refracturing of surrounding reservoir rock to improve diminished flow. Wells may be plugged and recompleted in a different level of producing sands or occasionally abandoned and redrilled. Salt water, frequently encountered and produced in considerable quantities with oil, must be disposed of—usually through reinjection wells to return it to the reservoir formation. Still another example of an operating problem which affects production costs, or life of the mine, is water encroachment in either shaft or pit mines which requires containment by methods such as pumping, construction of diversionary shafts or ditches, and cofferdams.

Sometimes, as a result of these operating problems, production is shut down before all reserves are exhausted because further exploitation becomes unprofitable or impossible. Similarly, development and production of a newly discovered mineral deposit may be deferred pending more favorable economic conditions.

Elements of production cost include royalties, exhaustion of capital facilities provided during the exploratory and development phases, depreciation of production equipment, maintenance of mine facilities and properties, direct and indirect labor, supplies, attendant supervisory and administrative overheads, and, in many states, the cost of restoring landscape destroyed by open-pit mining.

CHAPTER 2: EXTRACTIVE OPERATIONS

TABLE 4
Crude Ore and Total Material Handled at Surface and Underground Mines by Commodities in 1966 (Percent)

Commodity	Crude ore Surface	Crude ore Underground	Total material Surface	Total material Underground
Metals:				
Bauxite	90	10	93	7
Beryllium	100	......	100	......
Copper	86	14	95	5
Gold:				
Lode	39	61	79	21
Placer	100	......	100	......
Iron ore	91	9	95	5
Lead	......	100	3	97
Manganese ore	......	100	......	100
Manganiferous ore	100	......	100	......
Mercury	56	44	77	23
Molybdenum	19	81	51	49
Nickel	100	......	100	......
Rare-earth metals and thorium	100	......	100	......
Silver	42	58	35	65
Titanium: Ilmenite	100	......	100	......
Tungsten	......	100	......	100
Uranium	24	76	88	12
Zinc	3	97	7	93
Total	83	17	92	8
Nonmetals:				
Abrasives:				
Emery	100	......	100	......
Garnet	100	......	100	......
Tripoli	44	56	59	41
Asbestos	96	4	98	2
Barite	97	3	98	2
Boron minerals	100	......	100	......
Clays	97	3	99	1
Diatomite	100	......	100	......
Feldspar	100	......	100	......
Fluorspar	3	97	7	93
Graphite	100	......	100	......
Gypsum	75	25	88	12
Kyanite	100	......	100	......
Lithium minerals	100	......	100	......
Magnesite	100	......	100	......
Marl, greensand	100	......	100	......
Mica: Scrap	100	......	100	......
Olivine	100	......	100	......
Perlite	100	......	100	......
Phosphate rock	98	2	99	1
Potassium salts	......	100	......	100
Pumice	100	......	100	......
Salt	32	68	32	68
Sand and gravel	100	......	100	......
Sodium carbonate (natural)	......	100	......	100
Sodium sulfate (natural)	100	......	100	......
Stone:				
Crushed and broken	96	4	96	4
Dimension	95	5	94	6
Sulfur: Frasch-process mines	100	......	100	......
Talc, soapstone, and pyrophyllite	41	59	63	37
Vermiculite	100	......	100	......
Wollastonite	12	88	12	88
Total	96	4	97	3
Grand total	94	6	95	5

Source: United States Department of the Interior, *Minerals Yearbook 1966*, Volume I-II, 1967, p. 85.

Classification of Mineral Reserves

Mineral reserves in most extractive industries are classified according to the stage of development or the quality of the estimate regarding total reserves available. Although different terms are used to identify the classifications, three classifications are common: mineral reserves which can be produced with existing facilities are classified as "developed" reserves in the petroleum industry and as "proven" reserves in the other extractive industries; reserves which are known to exist but require additional expenditures for development before they can be produced are classified as "undeveloped-proven" reserves in the petroleum industry and as "probable" reserves in the other extractive industries; reserves which have not been sufficiently explored to provide reliable estimates of recoverable quantities are classified as "undeveloped-unproven" reserves in the petroleum industry and as "possible" reserves in the other extractive industries.

Joint Operations and Other Special Contractual Arrangements

Joint-operating agreements are arranged to divide the risk of exploration and development or to provide a more efficient means of developing and recovering minerals from a property in which more than one person has a working interest. Joint operations merit particular attention because they give rise to many complicated contractual arrangements involving relative participations in costs and output. This type of contractual arrangement is found most frequently in, but is not confined to, the petroleum industry.

Joint Exploration, Development, or Operating Arrangements. A joint-operating agreement provides the basis for sharing development and production costs and output among the cooperating persons. These activities may be carried out through either joint ventures, partnerships, or jointly owned corporations.

In a carried-interest arrangement, one owner (the "carrying interest") agrees to advance development costs for another (the "carried interest"). Amounts advanced are recoverable only from the carried interest's share of future production. If the carried interest is paid out (that is, when advances are fully recovered), the carried interest reverts to a full working interest participation in further production and development costs and revenue.

Profit-sharing interests participate in whatever profits might result from operations. They are distinguished from working interests by the absence of full participation in revenue and costs. Profit-sharing arrangements are usually made in connection with the acquisition of properties.

Other Special Contractual Arrangements. The petroleum industry is also a particularly prolific source of other contractual arrangements such as farm-outs and test-well contributions. In a farm-out, the owner or lessee assigns his mineral rights to another operator for exploration and development, retaining an overriding royalty or other type of economic interest. The second party, to whom this arrangement is a farm-in, receives an assignment of mineral rights in exchange for undertaking to drill wells.

A test-well contribution may or may not involve the transfer of fractional working interests. In its simplest form, the test-well contribution consists of an agreement to pay the owner of an adjacent tract for a portion of the cost of drilling an exploratory well on his property. The agreement may require contribution only when the well is unsuccessful (a dry-hole contribution), or it may require contribution regardless of outcome (a bottom-hole contribution). These contributions are regarded by most operators as exploration costs since their purpose is to obtain geological information bearing on the contributor's acreage from the drilling experience on a neighboring tract.

Minerals, particularly oil and gas, are frequently sold or otherwise committed in advance of production. These arrangements, known as carved-out production payments, are made as a means of financing the purchase of reserves or of maximizing allowable reductions in federal income taxes.

Other contractual arrangements common to the petroleum and other mining industries which give rise to problems in determining when revenue should be reported are take-or-pay contracts and agreements for sales of natural gas at rates not yet approved by the Federal Power Commission. In a take-or-pay contract, the buyer agrees to take or pay for a minimum quantity of minerals each year. Usually, any amount paid in excess of the price of minerals taken is recoverable from future purchases in excess of minimum quantities. Contractual rate increases for natural gas sales regulated by the Federal Power Commission may be put into effect before approval by the Commission providing the supplier undertakes to refund any amounts later disallowed.

3

Basic Accounting Concepts and Principles Especially Applicable to Extractive Operations

22   Extractive operations are set apart from other industries by a common focus on the search for wasting natural mineral resources. In contrast with industries that seek to use a production process to increase economic utility by combining existing resources acquired in market exchanges, extractive industries search for natural resources with an intrinsic economic utility independent of the nature, cost, or market value of the resources used to discover them. This feature of extractive operations is unique.

Other characteristics of extractive operations significant to financial reporting include the following:

1. Mineral reserves, for the most part, are difficult to find, require relatively long periods for development before revenue can be realized, and require substantial expenditures in all phases of operations: discovery (including prospecting, acquisition, and exploration), development, and production.

2. Discovery costs bear little or no predictable relationship to the potential market value of the minerals found.

3. Large amounts of discovery expenditures and significant amounts of development expenditures are unproductive.

4. Risk and tax considerations relating to discovery and transfer of mineral rights encourage complicated contractual arrangements affecting transfer and sharing of ownership and operations.

The basic concepts and accounting principles of financial reporting should be applied with due regard for the foregoing circumstances if meaningful financial reports on extractive operations are to be obtained. Accounting concepts and principles especially relevant to extractive operations are described in this chapter; each is referenced to the key accounting decisions which are discussed more fully in subsequent chapters.

Basic Accounting Concepts and Principles

In the past, financial statements have been frequently regarded as merely a report to investors and others on the stewardship of the resources of an enterprise, since they report historical facts and do not attempt to show the value of the enterprise. Investors, however, use financial statements not only as a report on stewardship but also as an aid to predicting the future trend of operations. The latter purpose has assumed primary importance in recent years. Although historical cost and past events are the primary basis of financial statements, future events play an important role in the preparation of financial statements in that predictions of future events are used in classifying and evaluating the effects of expenditures. If the future effects of unusual events and conditions are not recognized and disclosed, financial statements standing alone may give rise to erroneous inferences as to future trends in operations.

Thus expenditures which are expected to benefit future operations should be capitalized and matched against related revenue; expenditures which are not expected to benefit future operations should be expensed. Probability plays a role in making the decision: a relatively high degree of probability of future benefit justifies, and requires, capitalization of expenditures; a relatively low degree of probability of future benefit requires a charge to current expense.

The dividing line between a relatively low degree of probability and a relatively high degree of probability cannot be drawn with precision. Informed, objective judgment should determine what best serves the interests of the persons using the financial report. An overly optimistic picture of financial position and results of operations would be unfair to investors; conversely, an unwarrantedly pessimistic view would also be unfair.

Three basic conventions of financial reporting are especially relevant to this study: the cost basis for reporting assets, the realization basis for reporting revenue, and the concept of conservatism. The matching process is an important corollary to the realization convention; recognition of revenue only at the point of sale requires that related costs must be deferred. Costs (efforts) will then be reported as expense in the same period as the results of those efforts.

Cost Basis for Financial Statements

The structuring of financial statements on the basis of the cost convention requires, first, recognition and measurement of cost and, second, identification of the effort represented by cost incurred with results obtained in the form of revenue.

Cost is a measure of effort. It is recognized when an exchange has taken place. Cost is ordinarily the result of an expenditure of cash or cash equivalent, but it can also arise in an exchange that consists of assumption by the purchaser of an obligation or commitment to expend equivalent assets in future periods. Thus, cost is defined as:

> ... the amount, measured in money, of cash expended or other property transferred, capital stock issued, services performed, or a liability incurred, in consideration of goods or services received or to be received.[1]

The cost convention requires that expenditures (including obligations and commitments) be carried at the equivalent exchange price at the time of incurrence. No recognition is given to changing value of the currency. Although cost is usually the fairest measure of effort at the time of incurrence, it may not fully measure effort at the time revenue is realized, especially if periods of inflation intervene between expenditure and realization. The problem of restating financial statements for general price-level changes is covered in *APB Statement 3*, which was issued in June 1969, and is therefore not considered further in this study.

Under the cost concept, accumulations of expenditures which benefit future periods are reported as assets. They do not purport to repre-

---

[1] *Accounting Terminology Bulletin No. 4*, "Cost, Expense and Loss," 1957 p. 1.

sent current value (except when realizable market value is less than cost—an application of the convention of conservatism). Expenditures which benefit current revenue or which cannot be demonstrated as having benefit for the future are expensed.

Determination of the appropriate measure of cost in extractive operations is important in accounting for several types of transactions peculiar to extractive operations. (These transactions are discussed more fully in Chapter 6.) It is important in the exchange of mineral properties by an ABC transaction in which the consideration paid by the purchaser is part cash and part obligation to produce in the future a portion of mineral reserves for the account of the seller; and in recording farm-outs and carried-interest arrangements by which the potential benefit of a partial interest in mineral reserves accrues to one participant as the result of effort by another. Also, conveyances of continuing fractional interests in mineral properties raise questions of measurement of the cost of the remaining portion of the original interest: Are the proceeds from conveyances properly a reduction of cost of the original investment, or more properly revenue to which a portion of the cost of the original interest should be attached?

Although financial reports are essentially a historical representation of operations containing implications for the future, the cost basis may not provide sufficiently informative reports on extractive operations. The discovery of mineral reserves produces resources which have a potential market value with an uncertain relationship to discovery cost. In these circumstances, is it reasonable and fair to the investor to report as assets only the costs attached to the discovery or should the potential market value of the mineral resources be recorded as an asset? This question, which deals with the relevancy of both the cost convention and the realization convention to the extractive industries, is discussed in Chapter 8.

Realization Convention

The realization convention specifies the point in the cycle of operations at which results of enterprise activities are to be recognized.

> The problem of allocation of income to particular short periods obviously offers great difficulty—indeed, it is the point at which conventional treatment becomes indispensable, and it must be recognized that some conventions are scarcely in harmony with the facts. Manifestly, when a laborious process of manufacture and sale culminates in the delivery of the product at a profit, that profit is

not attributable, except conventionally, to the moment when the sale or delivery occurred. The accounting convention which makes such an attribution is justified only by its demonstrated practical utility.[2]

The convention that revenue should be recognized only at the time of sale (and, then, only if earned) foregoes realization of profit until almost the last process in the chain of effort which leads to revenue. Yet it has to be acknowledged that the market value created by combining resources during a manufacturing or similar process is really earned gradually as effort is expended. The realization convention avoids recognition of revenue and profits which may not materialize because of market uncertainties. The convention produces a reasonable approximation of economic results when there is a steady flow of product in all stages of completion at any one time; it may materially distort economic results when there is an assured market or when the production process extends over more than one reporting period. In those circumstances, the realization convention is sometimes modified so that revenue recognized more accurately reflects economic results.

Thus, the realization convention is modified when profit from long-term construction contracts is recognized on a percentage-of-completion basis. This basis of reporting recognizes revenue as resources are combined through the production process.

The realization convention is also modified when precious metal inventories are carried at realizable market prices. If there is an assured market at a fixed price (gold, for example), recognizing revenue at the completion of the manufacturing process is accepted as a more meaningful representation of results of operations.[3]

The accounts of open-end investment companies are accorded similar treatment with regard to inventories of marketable securities which are carried at quoted market prices. Still other examples exist in meat packing and nursery operations in which items processed or grown for sale are carried at net realizable market prices.

Each of these exceptions illustrates that the realization convention depends for its usefulness and acceptance upon the reasonableness of results in particular circumstances. In those situations in which the realization convention is modified, however, certain compelling or mitigating factors must be present. These include: (1) the availability

---

[2] George O. May, *Financial Accounting*, 1943, p. 30.
[3] *Accounting Research Bulletin No. 43*, 1953, Chapter 4, par. 16.

of accurate measurements of asset changes, (2) the possible distortion of periodic income by use of the sale basis (particularly for long-term construction contracts), or (3) the occurrence of the critical event in enterprise activities before a sale occurs thereby making the sale perfunctory (particularly for precious metals and marketable securities of investment companies). Usually more than one of the factors cited must apply in a particular circumstance to justify a departure from the sale basis.

Despite the exceptions cited, the realization rule continues to be the normal basis for recognition of revenue. In every case there is a general presumption that the sale basis of revenue recognition is appropriate, and deviations must be supported by evidence of its shortcomings. This presumption is strengthened by the terms of a rule adopted by the membership of the AICPA in 1934 and reprinted in Chapter 1A of *ARB 43*, issued in 1953.

> 1. Unrealized profit should not be credited to income account of the corporation either directly or indirectly.... Profit is deemed to be realized when a sale in the ordinary course of business is effected, unless the circumstances are such that the collection of the sale price is not reasonably assured. An exception to the general rule may be made in respect of inventories in industries (such as packing-house industry) in which owing to the impossibility of determining costs it is a trade custom to take inventories at net selling prices, which may exceed cost.

The realization convention comes to grips with the problem of the type of evidence needed before accounting entries can be made. The evidence must be convincing and have a high degree of certainty. The sale basis meets these requirements; it yields verifiable and objective amounts, amounts that can be corroborated by persons other than the preparer and that are free from bias. The sale basis may be abandoned and alternatives used in connection with recording revenue only if another basis meets the standards of accuracy of estimate and reliability of evidence or if the sale basis produces large irregularities in the timing and amount of recognition of revenue that do not reflect the underlying continuity of enterprise activities. An example of the former exception is found in accounting for precious metals at selling price,[4] while the latter exception is exemplified in accounting for long-term construction contracts. *ARB 45*, issued in October 1955, discusses

---

[4] *Ibid.*

the percentage-of-completion method for construction contracts as follows:

> 7. The principal advantages of the percentage-of-completion method are periodic recognition of income currently rather than irregularly as contracts are completed, and the reflection of the status of the uncompleted contracts provided through the current estimates of costs to complete or of progress toward completion.
>
> 8. The principal disadvantage of the percentage-of-completion method is that it is necessarily dependent upon estimates of ultimate costs and consequently of currently accruing income, which are subject to the uncertainties frequently inherent in long-term contracts.

ARB 45 (paragraph 15) generally recommends the percentage-of-completion method, but states that the completed contract method should be used if dependable estimates are lacking or inherent hazards cause the forecasts to be doubtful.[5]

The excerpts from *ARB 45* give some indication of the criteria that can be applied to exceptions to realization on the sale basis. The advantages of a departure from the sale basis can outweigh the uncertainties of estimates. Apparently, in the case of long-term construction contracts, the advantages of periodic recognition of income and reflection of the status of uncompleted contracts outweigh the disadvantages of estimates. Note also that the contract or sale price is known in a long-term construction contract and that it is total cost rather than total revenue that is in doubt.

The circumstances of extractive operations suggest that the usefulness of the realization convention has to be carefully considered. The objective of extractive operations is the discovery of natural resources with an intrinsic value which may eventually be recovered through production and sale. Although substantial expenditures are committed to discovery, development, and production, the ultimate sale price reflects realization not only of costs incurred but also of discovery value, the premium in price that the market places upon the intrinsic value of the mineral resource. The significance of discovery value as a component of the final sale price varies among the extractive industries and among different forms of organization. For example, if the mineral resource is plentiful, as in sand and gravel operations, the discovery value is relatively minor (as evidenced by the sale of properties at farmland prices); if it is scarce, as in petroleum or metals, the discovery value is greater.

---

[5] See also *ARB 43*, Chapter 11A, par. 13.

The relative importance of the discovery value of the mineral to the investor is also affected by whether the mineral resource is to be produced and sold to independent processors and fabricators or whether it is to be transferred to other departments of the organization as the raw material for further processing and refining. To the investor, discovery values of mineral reserves in a vertically integrated company may not be as significant as in a company which is engaged solely in exploration and production. The use value (as a raw material) of mineral reserves to a processor may be more significant than market value. Mineral reserves, however, are important to all extractive operations, and their potential market or use values, for the most part, cannot be measured appropriately by the accumulated expenditures for discovery and development. Despite that fact, the realization convention has been followed in reporting on extractive operations; discovery values have not been recorded until a sale occurs.

The realization convention is especially relevant to the sale of carved-out production payments in which future production is sold in current periods, to revenue from sale of minerals under take-or-pay contracts or from gas sales under temporary rate orders, and to the question of how to present to investors the resources represented by mineral reserves not yet mined. (Discussed in Chapters 6 and 8.)

Matching Process

The basic idea in the matching process is that cause-and-effect relationships between cost and revenue must be recognized in financial reporting to produce a meaningful comparison of effort and result in particular reporting periods. Expenditures which can be identified as an element in the cost of a product ultimately sold should be reported as expense in the same period as the revenue. Expenditures that cannot be related to specific revenue but can be related to particular accounting periods should be reported as expense in the appropriate periods. This matching process is essential in presenting fairly the results of operations and the financial position of the enterprise when revenue is recognized at the time of sale.

The ability to identify expenditures with specific revenue varies. Little difficulty is involved in accounting for expenditures which have an observable, objective physical relationship to a product or service; for example, direct materials and direct labor, or to a particular period, for example, selling expenses. Similarly, there is little difficulty in the identification process when expenditures are patently worthless. Between these two extremes, however, lies an area containing various degrees of uncertainty in identification of expenditures with specific revenue or periods. Matching of costs with particular revenue or periods in this gray area can be accomplished only by conventions which are generally accepted because they produce a reasonable result.

Many costs other than direct labor and direct material are so closely associated with the process of manufacturing a product that they are commonly identified with the product and become part of its assigned cost. Most indirect manufacturing costs fall in this category. In the absence of a direct physical relationship to product, such as exists with direct materials and direct labor, attachment of indirect manufacturing costs to specific products requires the use of cost centers. Cost centers provide the medium by which the relationship can be drawn between cost incurred and benefit obtained in terms of completed product.

Cost centers may be constructed from areas of activity, from separate processes, or from organizational responsibilities (the product itself, of course, is also a cost center). Circumstances affect the form of cost center but all should result in consistent, objective, and logical product costs: consistent in producing a similar answer in similar circumstances; objective in being free of bias; and logical in the assumed effort/result relationship.

It is acceptable to reflect in the final product cost all expenditures identified with a cost center to the extent that they are normal and necessary. Thus, product and material spoilage, idle man or machine time, and idle facility costs may properly be included in finished product cost if they are normal. However, this is an economic relationship rather than a direct benefit relationship, and therefore the same costs should be expensed if they are abnormal in amount.

Indirect costs which cannot reasonably be identified with cost centers are expensed on a period basis either because they are unproductive or because they are more logically identifiable with the overall business enterprise than with individual cost centers. Thus, the president's salary is rarely allocated to product cost. Similarly, expenditures which result in general, rather than specific, benefits to the enterprise are normally charged to expense on a period basis. Examples are general office expenses, advertising, and general research.

The size of the cost center can affect the amount of costs deferred to future periods and the amount of cost assigned to each product unit. A broad view, resulting in large cost centers encompassing many individual expenditures and more than one separate process or product, tends to result in assigning more expenditures to product cost, largely because of the view that all normal expenditures in a cost center are properly a part of product cost. In contrast, cost centers restricted to single processes or single products with closely identifiable costs tend to result in a lesser proportion of total cost assigned to product. Furthermore, variations in size of cost center will affect the average cost of product since the relationship between the two critical factors of cost input and product output differs.

The matching process is especially difficult in extractive operations. The relationship between expenditure and result is uncertain, and the interval for exploitation of discoveries is lengthy. Prospecting and acquisition costs are expended for a long-range potential benefit, not presently identifiable; exploration costs are mostly nonproductive; development costs are frequently nonproductive and when successful are recoverable through sale of reserves over relatively long periods of time during which many changes can occur in the factors affecting economic recoverability of the minerals. Other features of extractive operations also create special matching problems: mine restoration costs; advance and minimum royalties; costs of reinjected hydrocarbons; and the allocation of total cost to joint-product minerals. These items are discussed in Chapters 4 and 5.

Conservatism

The essence of financial reporting to shareholders is to report expenditures and revenue in proper relation to each other so as to bring about an appropriate correlation of effort and result. Each set of financial statements, therefore, includes some element of prediction concerning the eventual outcome of expenditures and, in some cases, revenue.

If the results of each effort were obvious, there would be no reason to express the facts in any manner other than the evident result. However, reasonably objective and verifiable facts as to future events are not always obtainable.

Any financial report reflects various degrees of uncertainty regarding future events, a condition which intensifies as the degree of risk inherent in the operations increases. If there is uncertainty as to whether future revenue will result from current expenditures, the question must be raised whether ultimate usefulness should be attributed to the expenditures by capitalizing them or whether the outcome is so uncertain that they should be charged to expense currently in order not to promise too much to the investor.

In retrospect, events demonstrate what the proper accounting treatment of these expenditures should have been; but current financial reports cannot be based on certainty as to future events, only on judgment as to what the events will probably be. Consequently, management's assessment of the degree of probability of future benefit resulting from current expenditures is an important element in determining what expenditures should be capitalized and deferred and what expenditures should be charged to expense currently.

The matching process is made difficult by these uncertainties as to future events. Accordingly, the concept of conservatism promotes a more consistent application of the matching concept in situations in which the facts are uncertain. In a sense, therefore, the concept of conservatism is a limiting convention that is intended to protect the investor against an unwarrantedly optimistic financial report. It is not intended to be used in a manner which would produce an unwarrantedly pessimistic report. Conservatism dictates only that if the facts are in doubt the less favorable viewpoint should be adopted. The essence of the conservatism convention is expressed in *Accounting Research Study No. 7:*

> ... a quality of judgment to be exercised in evaluating the uncertainties and risks present in a business entity to assure that reasonable provisions are made for potential losses in the realization of recorded assets. ...[6]

Conservatism in financial reporting assumes greater importance as future events become less predictable. The risks involved in extractive operations, in the first instance, as to whether any minerals will be discovered and, subsequently, as to whether they can be produced at a profit, are sufficiently great to require careful consideration of the conservatism convention.

Accounting for Income Taxes

Tax laws and regulations recognize the unusual features of extractive operations by requiring or permitting many transactions to affect

---

[6] Paul Grady, "Inventory of Generally Accepted Accounting Principles for Business Enterprises," 1965, p. 35.

taxable income in periods other than those in which they affect financial statement income. Some of the resulting differences between net taxable income and income before taxes for financial statement purposes are permanent differences whereas others are temporary. Furthermore, an interplay of permanent and temporary tax differences for extractive companies creates an amorphous class of items which are partly permanent and partly temporary.

Accounting Principles Board Opinion No. 11, "Accounting for Income Taxes," issued in December 1967, requires interperiod income tax allocation of the tax effect of timing (temporary) differences but not of permanent differences. The Opinion specifically mentions excess of percentage over cost depletion as a permanent difference not requiring interperiod tax allocation. The Opinion also mentions the possibility that other differences between book and tax income in extractive operations, including those resulting from the treatment of intangible drilling and development costs, may be permanent in effect. These and other tax differences are discussed in Chapter 7.

Disclosure

Reconciling the varied uses to which financial statements are put with their essentially historical nature would be difficult, if not impossible, without supplementary comments. Notes describing accounting practices and events and circumstances important to interpretation of the financial statements are an integral part of the report. Supplementary financial and statistical data, not necessarily in monetary terms, are frequently furnished to provide additional information on operations.

Neither the Accounting Principles Board nor the predecessor committee on accounting procedure has issued a comprehensive pronouncement on what information should be disclosed either in explanatory notes to financial statements or in other parts of annual reports. Disclosure requirements, however, are contained in several accounting research bulletins and APB Opinions.

The rules and regulations that apply to financial reports and prospectuses filed with the Securities and Exchange Commission contain the most comprehensive and authoritative set of disclosure requirements. In promulgating its rules and regulations, the Commission is motivated by its responsibility to assure that financial reports and prospectuses on file with the agency contain all the information necessary for an investor to make a prudent investment decision. Most people would agree that the same general objective of disclosure should apply to annual reports to shareholders, although they would not necessarily agree with the specific disclosure requirements of the SEC.

Some disclosure information is qualitative; for example, descriptions of accounting principles when alternative practices are available and disclosure of judgmental choices affecting the application of principles (consolidation practices, service lives of properties, actuarial assumptions for pensions, inventory costing methods, etc.). These qualitative disclosure items are probably not essential but they are useful in comparing the financial statements with those of other companies.

Other disclosure items are quantitative; for example, disclosure of contingent unrecorded assets and liabilities and significant events affecting current operations which might not be expected to occur with similar impact in future periods. An investor should be informed of those events which might affect future operations in a way that cannot be deduced from current financial statements. Information of this nature is essential to an evaluation of the financial statements.

Annual reports contain other disclosure information, not directly related to the financial statements, to inform investors more fully of the company's level of activity. Thus, many companies present resource and operating information not necessarily expressed in financial terms; for example, production capacity, research and development activities, new products, changes in markets, and physical operating data on volumes produced, processed, or marketed.

Ideally, disclosure should compensate for the limitations of financial statements as a means of evaluating company operations, whether for one year or a number of years, and comparing the company's operations with others. Practically, even the best disclosure will not be able to overcome completely the basic limitations necessarily imposed on financial statements by the conventional nature of accounting principles, the segmentation of continuing operations into arbitrary reporting periods, the uncertainties of transactions not yet completed, and the many other facets of complex operations which do not fit easily into financial terms or financial presentations. What is appropriate in some circumstances may be inappropriate in others. Disclosure must fit the individual situation; judgment rather than specific rules for disclosure should prevail.

The variety of circumstances in extractive operations, the complicated accounting problems, and the existence of substantial mineral resources not reflected in the balance sheet indicate the need for careful consideration of disclosure requirements in financial reports on extractive operations. Chapter 8 contains recommendations for disclosure.

Reporting Unit

Selection of the reporting unit is important to informative financial reporting if related operations are carried out through more than one legal entity. Parent company statements are useful for some purposes but have only limited significance to investors if important operations are conducted by controlled subsidiaries. In these circumstances, consolidated financial statements have for some time been considered the most useful form of presentation to portray the operations of the enterprise as a whole.

More recently, equity accounting has become generally accepted for investments in controlled domestic subsidiaries which are not consolidated.[7] The practice of equity accounting is being extended in some cases to jointly owned companies with relatively few owners, especially when the jointly owned operations are an integral part of the operations of the owners. Some companies, however, continue to carry these investments on the cost basis.

Extension of extractive operations through joint ventures and jointly owned corporations is common. The high risk and heavy capital characteristics of the industry promote this type of arrangement. Many of these operations are no different in character from those that are carried out directly by the owner or through controlled subsidiaries. It is not common practice, however, for extractive companies to report investments in jointly owned corporations on an equity basis.

Joint ownership of extractive operations is sufficiently common to require consideration of appropriate financial reporting. The American Institute of Certified Public Accountants, however, now has in process a research study on intercorporate investments. No recommendations on this subject are included in this research study because the accounting principles developed for industry generally are also expected to apply to the extractive industries.

---

[7] *APB 10,* December 1966, par. 3.

Summary

The basic concepts and principles of financial reporting must be applied appropriately to the distinguishing characteristics of extractive operations. Most of these characteristics are related to the unique features of a wasting natural resource which has a potential market value largely unrelated in any predictable measure to costs incurred for discovery. Expenditures are substantial, recovery periods are long, and risk is great.

Particular attention must be given to measurement of cost, to recognition of revenue, to selection of meaningful cost centers, and to disclosure of mineral resources.

4

The Capital/Expense Decision

The operations of extractive industries, described in Chapter 2, involve many transactions that not only contain potential benefit to future operations but also involve complexities that obscure identification with specific periods. This chapter describes present practice regarding the capital/expense decision and develops recommendations to improve those practices.

The matching process requires that expenditures which can be identified with future rather than current revenue should be deferred to the periods expected to benefit. In the extractive industries, the presence of economically recoverable reserves is essential to a decision to capitalize expenditures. Whether reserves exist and the extent of recoverable reserves are questions of fact not determinable until the discovery and development phases of operations are fairly well advanced.

Recovery of minerals is a gradual process that begins with the hope of discovery during the prospecting stage, reaches an assumption in the exploration stage, and proceeds to a relatively high degree of probability during development. Accounting for expenditures in each of these stages requires that they be tested against the question of whether the degree of probability of inventory-in-place is sufficiently high to justify representing to the investor that current expenditures should be carried forward to future periods. Probability, of course, becomes less as risk increases—and these are high-risk industries.

This analysis suggests that:

1. Costs of prospecting which do not immediately establish

the presence of minerals-in-place should be charged to expense as incurred.

2. Exploration costs should be deferred only if the presence of economically recoverable reserves is indicated; otherwise they should be charged to expense as incurred.

3. Costs of developing reserves for future production should be deferred and matched against future revenue.

These presumptions reflect the fact that all activities of a mining company, in the phases of operations under study, are directed ultimately to the finding and production of mineral reserves and that the justification for representing expenditures as assets to be carried forward as charges against future operations depends on the ability to identify particular expenditures with specific reserves. Direct association of particular expenditures with specific economically recoverable reserves requires that the expenditures be carried forward to the period in which the reserves are produced. Lack of direct association between particular expenditures and specific reserves which are economically recoverable requires that the expenditures be charged to expense as incurred.

SURVEY OF PRESENT PRACTICES

Accounting for Prospecting Costs

The costs incurred during the prospecting phase of extractive operations comprise:

1. Geological and geophysical costs—for example, salaries, equipment, supplies and related indirect expenses of geologists, scouts, and other employees, or payments to outside contractors for initial geological studies; reconnaissance surveys and tests of the earth's structures; payments to landowners for rights of access to make further tests (shooting rights).

2. Options to acquire mineral rights.

Geological and Geophysical Costs. The major part of geological and geophysical costs is charged to expense as incurred. Some companies do not capitalize any geological and geophysical costs; others defer the costs directly identifiable with specific properties being explored and, if the property is acquired, capitalize the deferred costs as part of undeveloped property cost. The portion directly identifiable with specific properties is ordinarily a relatively small part of total geological and geophysical costs.

The tendency to regard geological and geophysical costs as period charges is more pronounced when they are incurred by the company's own force than when they are paid to outside contractors. Furthermore, more indirect costs tend to be capitalized when outside contractors are used. The definition of costs of the company's own force directly attributable to the acquisition of properties is relatively narrow and tends to be confined to direct-cost items. Payments to outsiders, on the other hand, reflect both direct and indirect costs of the contractor.

Prospecting costs are not significant in industries producing relatively common minerals such as coal, sand, stone, and limestone. Expenditures for prospecting in these industries are generally expensed regardless of whether acreage is retained. In stone, sand, and gravel operations, prospecting and exploration are frequently classified as marketing expense. The marketing function has the responsibility for locating suitable deposits sufficiently close to construction work to permit competitive bidding. Proximity is important because transportation cost is a major element.

A survey of petroleum industry accounting practices shows that approximately 56% of the respondents capitalize costs of outside crews related to acreage acquired and retained, whereas only 17% of the respondents capitalize costs of their own crews related to acreage acquired and retained.[1] Similar results were obtained in an earlier study made by Horace R. Brock.[2] Professor Brock's study of 61 petroleum companies shows that geological and geophysical costs identifiable with acreage retained were capitalized by 62% of the companies employing outside crews, but by only 23% of the companies using their own staff.

---

[1] American Petroleum Institute, *Report of Certain Petroleum Industry Accounting Practices,* 1965, pp. 21-22, 26.

[2] "Petroleum Accounting," *The Journal of Accountancy,* December 1956, pp. 53-67.

Professor Brock concluded that smaller companies capitalize a greater part of prospecting and preliminary exploration costs than do larger companies. He attributed this, in part, to greater reluctance to depart from income tax accounting and greater materiality of amounts. Both the Brock study and the API study indicate that the larger portion of geological and geophysical costs in the petroleum industry is charged to operations and that outside contract costs are capitalized more frequently than costs of the company's own staff.

The tendency to charge geological and geophysical costs to operations as they are incurred is responsive to the following factors: (1) the flow of geological and geophysical expenditures is relatively steady and is a normal continuing cost of staying in business; (2) the expenditures are preliminary and serve the broad purpose of initially defining areas of general interest and then identifying particular prospects within the areas of general interest for intensive exploration; and (3) expenditures are unlikely to produce future revenue since most prospects surveyed prove unproductive. In fact, an analogy is frequently drawn between geological and geophysical costs and research costs in an industry of similarly high risk.

For tax purposes, geological and geophysical costs which lead to acquisition of particular properties must be capitalized. As the tax rules are applied, frequently only outside contract costs are required to be capitalized. The tax requirement undoubtedly influences some companies to follow the same practice for financial accounting purposes, particularly smaller companies which are more inclined to keep their accounts on the tax basis.

The API survey and the Brock study found that more petroleum companies capitalized outside contract costs than capitalized costs of their own force. Brock attributed this disparity to the fact that it is more difficult to identify own-force costs than outside contract costs, with particular units of property acquired. This is a reasonable explanation. Another reasonable explanation may be that outside contract costs are more likely to represent unusual amounts because occasional efforts above the normal flow of prospecting activity are likely to be carried out by special contract. Many firms which expense the costs of their own force may capitalize amounts paid to outside contractors to avoid irregular impacts on results of operations.

The relative amounts of geological and geophysical costs ultimately capitalized by companies which follow the practice of capitalizing these costs are affected by the choice of prospect unit with which to identify these costs. Most companies define a prospect in terms of geographical areas of interest. The geological and geophysical costs identified with a given area of interest are capitalized or charged to expense according to the results of the prospecting effort and the company's policy. When suspected mineral formations are discovered in an area of interest and further exploration is intended, some or all prospecting costs assigned to that area of interest may be deferred pending further exploration. There is no consensus on this point in practice.

A relatively new minority practice that is gaining some popularity, particularly among smaller petroleum companies, is to capitalize all geological and geophysical costs (as well as exploration and development costs) regardless of results. This practice is based on the so-called "full-cost" or "total-cost" concept. At least 20 companies in the United States and Canada base their accounting on this concept. The distinctive feature of this treatment is to regard company-wide activities as one unit. The theory advanced is that all finding and development costs are part of an overall effort, the sum of which is expended for whatever result may be obtained. Accordingly, the entire cost of the program should be attributed to whatever is found. The method resembles a process-cost system in which all costs are attributed to unspoiled units. The ratio of successes to failures is much higher in a process-cost system, however.

Options to Acquire Mineral Rights. Options to acquire mineral rights by lease or purchase (frequently including land rights as well) are usually taken during the preliminary stages of exploration, and accordingly are included within the prospecting function in this research study. The cost of an option is ordinarily deferred until the decision is made to exercise or drop the option. When an option is exercised, the cost is usually capitalized as part of acquisition cost of the mineral rights; when an option is dropped, the cost is charged to expense (except by companies which subscribe to the full-cost concept).

Summary of Practices. To summarize accounting practices for prospecting costs:

1. Some companies capitalize that portion of geological and geophysical costs directly identifiable with acquisition

or retention of property rights, especially when the prospecting work is carried out by outside contract.

2. Some companies charge all geological and geophysical costs to expense as incurred, especially when the prospecting work is carried out by the company's own force.

3. Most companies defer the cost of options to acquire properties and later capitalize those that are exercised.

4. A small minority capitalize all prospecting costs (under the full-cost concept).

Accounting for Acquisition Costs

Property rights (mineral or mineral and surface) are acquired by lease or purchased in fee. Costs of acquisition include lease bonus and lease extension costs, purchase price, lease brokers' commissions, abstract and recording fees, filing and patenting fees, title search and other legal expenses, and costs of land and lease departments. Various carrying costs are incurred after acquisition but before production to hold property rights, for example, delay rentals, shut-in royalties, minimum royalties to lessors which might or might not be recoverable from future production, legal costs for title defense, and *ad valorem* taxes on unmined reserves prior to production. Acquisition costs also include geological and geophysical costs and options on acquired properties capitalized during the prospecting phase. Capitalized acquisition costs relate to the mineral reserves themselves and are subject to depletion as the reserves are mined.

Except for carrying costs, acquisition costs paid to outsiders are ordinarily capitalized. Inside acquisition costs, such as title search and other legal expenses, and land and lease department expenses are nearly always charged to expense as incurred. Carrying costs are usually charged to expense as incurred. Typical balance sheet captions for capitalized costs are "Leaseholds," "Coal lands and real estate," "Mine properties," and "Mineral deposits." An intermediate account such as "Undeveloped leases" may be used until the property is proven and the cost is reclassified or written off.

The cost of obtaining extension of a lease that otherwise would terminate is reported in one of two ways. Some companies which consider the event as two transactions—abandoning the old lease and entering a new one—capitalize the extension cost and write off acquisition costs carried for the expiring lease. Other companies add the cost of lease extensions to the existing capitalized lease costs. Professor Brock found a majority of petroleum companies writing off the old lease costs, but he queried only 24 of his subject companies on this point. The API survey did not include this item. For federal income tax purposes both the cost of the original lease and the cost of the extension must be capitalized.

Royalties and similar payments to retain exploration or mineral rights are substantial in amount and in complexity. They contain elements of both capital and expense, and the dominant characteristic is not always easily determinable. Nevertheless, most of the royalties and similar payments which may be classified as carrying costs (delay rentals, minimum payments, and other payments prior to production; minimum royalties in excess of those earned through production; and shut-in royalties extending the lease for one year or less) are charged to expense as incurred because they purportedly add no value to the property but result only in buying time or retaining rights.

Exceptions to general practice are made for minimum annual payments prior to production which are not avoidable by terminating the lease. Since the total amount must be paid regardless of whether the lease becomes a producer or is abandoned, many companies, perhaps a majority, handle these as a bonus paid on the installment basis and capitalize the amounts as they are paid. Other exceptions are sometimes made for unusually large royalties paid in advance of production which are recoverable from future production.

Legal costs for title defense, whether paid to outsiders or incurred by company staff, are charged to expense by a majority of the companies although there is a greater tendency to capitalize outside legal costs. *Ad valorem* taxes on mineral and surface lands prior to production are charged to operations as paid. In both these cases, the costs are viewed as a recurring expense of maintaining rights to minerals without adding anything of value.

All capitalized costs assigned to leasehold and mining rights are depletable for tax purposes, and cost depletion is seldom in excess of percentage depletion. The tax advantage lies with charging discretionary items to operations as expended. All other things being equal, therefore, one would expect to find reticence in capitalizing acquisition and carrying costs unless they relate to an item which is specifically required to be capitalized for tax purposes.

In the coal, metal, and nonmetal mining industries, and sometimes in the petroleum industry, both surface and mineral lands may be purchased, especially when strip mining is contemplated. In these cases a nominal value, if any, is assigned to the surface land. Income and expenses from the use of surface land for grazing, farming, or timber operations prior to stripping are included in current operations as a net item in other income or other expense.

An infrequent but interesting lease arrangement limits royalties payable out of current production to a maximum total amount. When the specified amount has been paid the lessee obtains perpetual rights to the minerals. Royalties paid are charged to operations despite the obvious analogy to an installment purchase.

Only 18 (all petroleum companies) of the 265 mining companies whose annual reports are reviewed in Chapter 8 disclosed the method of accounting for acquisition costs but none defined acquisition costs. Fifteen of these 18 petroleum companies reported capitalizing all acquisition costs (13 of which have adopted the full-cost concept). One company followed the opposite extreme of charging all acquisition costs to expense, and two reported a policy of capitalizing part of acquisition costs without specifying the items included.

To summarize accounting for acquisition and carrying costs of exploratory and mineral rights (in addition to prospecting and exploration costs which may have been capitalized):

1. Lease bonuses, lease extension costs, purchase price, lease brokers' commissions, abstract and recording fees, filing and patenting fees, and acquisition legal fees paid to outsiders are capitalized.

2. Delay rentals, shut-in royalties, minimum payments and royalties prior to production, inside acquisition and title defense legal costs, and *ad valorem* taxes on unmined reserves are charged to expense, except in the special situations covered in (3) and (4).

3. A significant number of companies capitalize minimum annual payments to lessors which are not avoidable by terminating the lease, and some companies defer unusually large minimum royalties which are recoverable from future production.

4. Some companies capitalize all acquisition costs (under the full-cost concept).

Accounting for Exploration Costs

Costs of exploration which lead to the retention and development of a mineral body are generally capitalized; costs of unsuccessful exploration are usually charged to operations. The cost of exploratory work in progress may be deferred until the prospect is proven, or may be charged to operations as incurred and retroactively capitalized in the event of success. When exploration costs are deferred, a provision for losses on probable failures is not customary except at year end and then only to the extent failures are known before the financial statements are issued. Dry-hole and bottom-hole contributions are usually charged to operations as incurred, although a large minority of companies capitalize these costs as part of the cost of nearby acreage when the test well is successful. The recipient credits these contributions to his drilling costs.

When an uneconomic discovery is made, the amount of exploration cost capitalized is sometimes limited to estimated recoverable amounts after taking into consideration expected further development and production costs.

In the petroleum industry, tangible costs and intangible drilling and development costs are accounted for separately. At one time it was common to charge all intangible drilling and development costs (IDC) to operations as incurred regardless of success; a few companies continue to follow this practice.

As mentioned in the discussion of prospecting costs, some companies capitalize all exploration effort regardless of result. The response from 32 companies in the API survey[3] included only one company which capitalized all exploration costs as a general policy regardless of result although four companies reported capitalizing costs of unsuccessful drilling below the lowest producing horizon in a well that is successful in a higher formation. Two companies reported that all IDC is charged to operations as incurred. The Brock study of 61 companies in 1956 turned up 15 which did not capitalize IDC on successful wells. Only one of the 61 companies capitalized IDC and tangible costs relating to unsuccessful wells.

Those companies which charge all IDC to operations as incurred cite conservatism (because IDC contains no salvageable values) and con-

---

[3] American Petroleum Institute, *Report of Certain Petroleum Industry Accounting Practices*, 1965, p. 26.

formity to income tax accounting as support. Their arguments regarding conservatism are set forth in the API study:

> The two companies that reported expensing intangible drilling costs applicable to successful wells stated that there should be no capitalization of items which, in themselves as intangibles, are nonrecoverable costs associated with the main business effort of the high-risk activities that characterize a production company.
>
> More specifically they said that all nonrecoverable costs, associated with the main business effort of those high-risk activities which characterize the work of production companies, should be charged to expense. This principle is unaffected by the size of the operation or whether the wells drilled turn out to be dry or productive. In addition, any charges to capital for eventual reflection on published statements should bear some reasonable relationship to the value of the assets represented at the date of acquisition. Intangible development costs do not qualify for such treatment.
>
> Also that the main reason for expensing these items is to avoid an understatement of current expenses and a consequent overstatement of earnings. The long-term trend for replacing oil reserves is one of continued higher costs, which reflect deeper drilling, less accessible areas, and fewer new large reservoirs, as well as the reduced purchasing power of the dollar. Finding and development costs of additional oil reserves today are generally far in excess of the current amortization per barrel.[4]

The one company in the API survey that capitalized all exploration costs argued that all expenditures, whether productive or nonproductive, should be amortized against the revenue obtained from reserves discovered as a result of the total exploratory effort to obtain a proper matching of revenue and cost (full-cost concept).

A few companies in extractive industries other than petroleum capitalize all exploratory costs, but none makes a distinction between tangible and intangible costs for accounting purposes.

In many extractive industries mining is carried out in successive stages. Exploration, development, and production operations are often in process simultaneously on the same property, and the nature of the costs is such that many of them cannot be associated clearly with future rather than current production.

---

[4] American Petroleum Institute, *Report of Certain Petroleum Industry Accounting Practices*, 1965, p. 26.

CHAPTER 4: THE CAPITAL/EXPENSE DECISION

An exploratory shaft driven to an ore deposit may become a main access shaft through which ore will be drawn as it is produced. Extensions of the main shaft or levels and cutting of stopes follow the receding face of the ore as it is mined. There is a continuous process of development that accompanies production. Although the cost of mining relates to the ore removed, it also provides access to additional ore. These circumstances differ from the drilling and equipping of an oil, gas, or sulfur well which will be producing over, say, the next 20 years. Because of the uncertainties involved in making a clear distinction between exploration and development costs on one hand and production costs on the other, the decision to capitalize successive exploration and development expenditures in a receding face mine is influenced by the stage of mining as much as by the nature of the expenditure. The exploratory stage ends and development begins at the point that a commercially recoverable reserve is determined to exist. The development stage ends when commercial production is obtained. It is unusual to capitalize additional exploration costs on a mine property after the development stage is reached, even though core drilling and other exploratory activities to define the limits of additional reserves are continued. Furthermore, early transition from the exploratory to the development stage is encouraged by income tax regulations which permit immediate charge-off of most development costs but restrict in some measure tax reductions from successful exploration costs, either by the statutory dollar limit or by recapture out of subsequent percentage depletion allowances.

The stage of mining in a petroleum operation has much less effect on the decision to capitalize expenditures. Additional wells are commonly drilled after commercial production of a petroleum reservoir begins, but the costs are capitalized if the well is successful to the same extent as costs of successful wells drilled prior to the production stage.

The review of annual reports for disclosure of accounting practices seems to bear out the methods stated above, but only sketchy information is given. Of the 265 companies, only 38 disclosed the basis of accounting for exploration costs, and the term was defined in only one instance. Of those 38 companies, 6 integrated and 7 nonintegrated petroleum companies reported capitalizing all exploration costs in line with the full-cost concept. One nonferrous metal company disclosed that it capitalizes all exploration costs and 2 nonferrous metal companies reported that they capitalize only outside exploration costs.

Twenty of the 38 companies disclosing the basis of accounting for exploration costs stated that they charged all exploration cost to expense as incurred. These companies are classified according to their primary activity as follows:

Primary Activity	Number
Integrated petroleum	4
Nonintegrated petroleum	10
Nonferrous metal	5
Salt, sulfur, and potash	1
	20

One nonintegrated petroleum company reported that it defers exploration costs related to reservations or licenses (large units) until the prospect is proven but that other exploration costs are charged to expense as incurred. Banff Oil Ltd., a nonintegrated producer, included the following statement in its 1964 annual report:

> All acquisition, exploration, rental and drilling costs are capitalized as non-producing properties. Costs relating to properties surrendered and costs of unproductive wells remain capitalized unless all properties within the related area are abandoned. If properties prove productive, the related costs are designated as producing properties.

The indication from the review of annual reports that 14 petroleum companies charged all exploration costs to expense may be misleading in the absence of a definition of exploration costs. It is not likely that any petroleum companies would charge successful exploratory drilling costs to income as incurred although they might well charge off all geological and geophysical, all unsuccessful drilling costs, all lease surrenders, and all delay rentals.

To summarize accounting for exploration costs:

1. Most companies capitalize successful exploration costs during the exploratory phase; a few petroleum companies make an exception for the IDC portion only.

2. Exploration costs incurred subsequent to the exploratory stage are rarely capitalized in industries other than petroleum.

3. A few companies, mostly in the petroleum industry, capitalize all exploration costs regardless of outcome (full-cost concept).

Differences in application of these general policies can affect the final relative amounts capitalized. For example, the definition of property unit used as a center for collecting costs to be written off as unsuccessful or capitalized and subsequently accounted for is quite significant; the smaller the unit, the less exploration cost tends to be capitalized.

Accounting for Development Costs

Development activities include: (1) drilling and equipping additional wells, driving shafts, and tunnels, (2) developing supporting material-handling and housing facilities and access roads, and (3) stripping overburden. Development costs include labor, supplies, and depreciation of construction and mining equipment or payments to contractors when the work is not done by the company's own force.

The nature of the expenditure is the controlling factor in deciding whether to capitalize development expenditures in industries such as petroleum or deep sulfur mining. The stage of mining is the more important factor in other mining industries in which operations are carried out in successive stages and include exploration and substantial development expenditures even after commercial production begins.

Petroleum Industry. Except for the minority practice of not capitalizing any of the IDC portion of exploration and development costs, expenditures for drilling and equipping petroleum development wells are capitalized when the wells are successful and are charged to expense when they are dry. Expenditures are usually carried as deferred charges until the status of the well is determined. Some companies capitalize all drilling costs in accordance with the full-cost concept regardless of the outcome.

Although Professor Brock found that 5 of the 61 companies he surveyed capitalized the cost of development dry wells whereas only one capitalized the cost of exploratory dry wells, the practice of differentiating between dry holes on unproven leases and dry holes on producing leases is not common. None of the companies in the API survey makes such a distinction for capitalizing purposes.

Other development expenditures in a proven petroleum field, such as expenditures for field storage tanks, roads, gathering systems, and natural gasoline plants, are capitalized and amortized to operations in accordance with the estimated life of the item or of the reserves, whichever is shorter.

Both farm-out and carried-interest arrangements are used to develop petroleum properties. In a farm-out the owner of the working interest in an undeveloped lease assigns it to a developer, retaining an economic but usually nonoperating interest. A variation of the farm-out calls for assignment of only part of the working interest in exchange for one or more "free" wells—wells drilled and equipped solely at the assignee's expense. In a carried-interest arrangement, the carrying partner develops and operates the property at his own risk. He is entitled to recover the portion of costs applicable to the carried interest out of any production before the carried partner begins to participate.

Accounting is substantially uniform for both farm-out and carried-interest arrangements. In a successful farm-out, the grantor transfers his capitalized undeveloped lease costs to the cost of the nonworking interest retained, or to the producing leasehold property account when a working interest in a free well is obtained. About 10% of the API survey respondents reported splitting the transferred costs attributed to a working interest in a free well. Their share of well equipment cost is charged to a depreciable equipment property account and the balance, if any, of their undeveloped leasehold cost is assigned to producing leaseholds. No entry is made for grantee development costs applicable to grantor's interest other than in memorandum accounts.

The other side of the farm-out arrangement—a farm-in—presents no unusual accounting problem. If the grantor retains a nonworking interest, the grantee need make no entries to reflect the situation other than to account for the grantor's overriding royalty interest in production as it is obtained. If the grantor retains a working interest under a free-well arrangement, the grantee records the portion of his free-well capital cost equivalent to the grantor's interest as a producing leasehold investment.

Since a carried-interest arrangement reverts to a normal fractional-interest participation once the carried costs have been recovered, at that point it no longer has any unique accounting significance of itself. Prior to payout, the carrying interest usually records the well and equipment costs as though no carried interests existed, keeping track of the status of the accounts of carried interests in memorandum records. As an alternative, some companies record the equity of the carried partner in these items as a receivable. Only one of the companies in the API group chose this alternative. This practice is defended on the grounds that the only right that the carrying partner has to the carried partner's share of revenue is the right to reimbursement from that revenue for costs and expenses advanced on behalf of the carried partner. Twenty-five companies in the API group follow the more prevalent practice of memorandum accounting for the carried interest. This majority practice conforms to the fact that the carried partner has only a contingent interest subject to payout which may never occur; he has no obligation or interest in development expenditures prior to payout.

Twenty-four petroleum companies reporting as carried partners were unanimous in making no entries in their accounts (other than memorandum) until after payout. In the meantime their property investment is carried at cost, to be amortized after payout is reached and their participation begins. They view the arrangement as an irrevocable assignment of their interest until after payout; transactions in which they have no interest should not be recorded.

Other Extractive Industries. A shift in perspective is needed in considering accounting practices for development of minerals which do not flow to the access facility as do oil and natural gas. As already observed, the stage of mining activity in these industries exerts a stronger influence on the decision to expense development expenditures as incurred or to carry them forward to future operations than does the nature of the expenditure. Development costs of a mine prior to the operating stage are usually capitalized, net of any revenue in the preoperating stage, and are amortized against production after commercial operations begin. Development costs after commercial operations begin are ordinarily charged off as incurred. The decision is usually made on a mine-by-mine basis if the amounts involved are substantial, but if a number of mines are in operation a normal level of development costs in a new mine may be charged off currently even though the mine is still in the preoperating stage.

Unusually large development costs incurred after the operating stage is reached may be deferred and amortized over several years. Extensive stripping costs are an illustration. Also, the cost of dams, ditches, and settling basins required in many mining industries may be deferred when built initially as a complete system. If subsequently extended as mining progresses, the additional costs are charged to operations.

The practice of charging development costs to operations as incurred after the operating stage of a mine has been reached is compatible with the practice of scheduling development expenditures in increments corresponding to the progress of production as mining facilities are extended. As mentioned previously, the Internal Revenue Code permits all development expenditures, except for oil and gas, to be deducted for tax purposes as incurred. This includes equipment expenditures otherwise of a capital nature which are incurred only to maintain current production (referred to as receding face costs).

The stage of mine development is used as a convenient reference point between expenditures which probably increase production and those which probably only maintain production. Presumably expenditures prior to the point of commercial production are made to obtain production from the entire mine, and expenditures to extend shafts, tunnels, levels, and stopes, together with track, wiring, ventilation, and similar costs after the preoperating phase are incurred chiefly to maintain production.

The preceding discussion refers to costs which are intangible or not salvageable. Movable, long-lived equipment and processing plants are customarily capitalized regardless of the stage of mine development.

Survey of Annual Reports. Mining company annual reports seem to provide slightly more information on development cost accounting practices than on exploration and acquisition costs. In the 265 annual reports reviewed in Chapter 8, the following information on accounting for development costs (defined in only one instance) was given:

Primary Activity	Total Number Reviewed	Capitalize All	Expense All	Capitalize Part
Integrated petroleum	54	6(a)	2	5
Nonintegrated petroleum	56	9(a)	3	8
Iron	25	—	—	—
Nonferrous metals	61	2	5	9(b)
Coal	18	—	—	2(b)
Bauxite, asbestos, and uranium	10	—	—	3(b)
Salt, sulfur, and potash	8	1	—	—
Cement, stone, gravel, and sand	33	—	—	—
	265	18	10	27

(a) Includes six integrated and seven nonintegrated petroleum companies following the full-cost concept.

(b) Indicated as being advance development or stripping costs.

Summary of Accounting Practices. The extent to which development expenditures are capitalized is influenced by (a) the nature of the item, (b) the result achieved, and (c) the stage of the mining process. The first two factors are critical in the petroleum and other well-mining industries while the last factor is critical in most other mining activities.

Thus, in the petroleum and other well-mining industries:

1. Successful development drilling and other expenditures, both tangible and intangible, are capitalized (but see (2) below); unsuccessful expenditures are charged to expense except for some companies on the full-cost concept.

2. A few petroleum companies continue the once common practice of capitalizing only the tangible cost portion of successful development expenditures and charging the intangible portion to expense as incurred.

3. The exchange of mineral interests for development work by others (farm-out and carried-interest arrangements) is recorded only in memorandum records.

In other mining industries:

1. Intangible costs are deferred if incurred prior to the production stage of the mining property.

2. Intangible and receding face costs incurred after the production stage is reached are charged to expense unless they are unusually extensive in relation to current production.

3. Movable equipment costs are usually capitalized.

Accounting for Production Costs

In addition to depletion, depreciation, and amortization of costs incurred and capitalized during the earlier stages of mining, production costs comprise labor and overhead, extensions of mining facilities and equipment, maintenance and repairs (including well work-overs), operating supplies, gas or other hydrocarbons purchased and re-injected for pressurization, restoration of landscaping in stripped areas, severance taxes, and royalties and other payments out of production.

The merging of development and production operations in mining by successive stages in hard-rock or surface mines has already been discussed. Except for that distinctive feature, mining operations in the production stage present the same type of accounting problems as in other industries. Although some of the costs are unique in their application to the mining process, the accounting decision to charge them off to expense as incurred or to defer them to future periods is made according to the nature of the expenditure and the degree to which it might benefit future as well as current production.

In general, the cost of equipment purchased or built during the production phase is allocated over its useful life or the life of the mine, whichever is shorter. It will be recalled from the discussion of development expenditures that a distinction is made with regard to expenditures for nonmovable facilities such as track and power lines, which maintain but do not increase production; these are charged to operations even though used during several years' operations. In some cases they may be deferred for short periods. An exception was noted in the limestone industry in which quarry track extensions are ordinarily capitalized; most quarry-materials handling, however, is now done by truck.

When open-pit mining methods are used, companies are frequently required to restore landscaping or convert exhausted mines to recreational use. Only a few companies provide for these restoration costs as mining progresses. The majority cite two reasons for not accruing restoration costs. First, restoration of landscaping is accomplished frequently with overburden removed from minerals about to be mined, in which case restoration costs are incurred and expensed as mining proceeds. Second, it is argued that the nonaccrual of restoration expense is offset by the nondeferral of stripping cost in advance of production.

Mining operations provide intriguing accounting questions involving inventories of ore in various stages of production. Extracted ore which has been crushed, sorted, cleaned, or otherwise processed to the point of shipment is obviously inventory and should be recorded as inventory. Proven reserves in the ground are also inventory in a sense although the related capitalized costs of acquisition, exploration, and development are ordinarily thought of as property costs. At any point in between, mineral is in various stages of removal. The stage may be as short as the trip from oil sand to field tank, or as long as it takes to cut and blast hard-rock ore, to load and bring it to the surface, and to crush, sort, screen, and concentrate or otherwise process it for shipment.

In most mining situations production is geared to sales, and ore is shipped as soon as it is produced. Inventories of the principal product tend to be low, but secondary minerals, necessarily produced because they occur in the same ore, may accumulate in mine-finished form. Sand is an illustration, since it frequently results as a by-product of gravel production.

Field stocks of oil and sulfur from flowing wells may or may not be carried as inventory. If the API survey is representative, about two-thirds of petroleum companies inventory field stocks. The remaining one-third maintains that production in advance of sales is not sufficiently material to justify inventory accounting.

A similarly mixed practice is reported to exist in the coal industries but unshipped coal stocks are usually quite small.

In underground-shaft or open-pit metal mining, ore is generally inventoried only after it has been concentrated, despite the fact that when block-caving mining methods are used substantial quantities of broken ore may lie in the mine and other quantities are in process of transportation or preliminary processing stages, such as crushing, sorting, and screening. Difficulties of estimating quantities are cited as the principal reason for not inventorying ore prior to concentration. Materiality is another contributing factor, for when large quantities of ore are stockpiled at a mill in anticipation of impossible mining conditions (as in heavy winter climates) they are usually inventoried to avoid distortion of operating results.

In nonmetal mining, ore is ordinarily inventoried at the mine site after the crushing, screening, sorting, and cleaning processes, but before the finishing processes, such as roasting, are started.

The elements of cost considered in inventory pricing tend to be limited to direct mining, initial treatment, and closely related overhead costs. Depreciation of capitalized lease and mine equipment costs and amortization of deferred development costs are included. General overhead, exploration costs, and depletion of capitalized mineral rights are usually excluded from inventory, except where depletion might be based on units produced rather than units sold, apparently a rare situation.

Pressure in oil reservoirs to facilitate production is often maintained by reinjection of gas produced with oil. Ultimately, when the maximum oil recovery has been obtained, the gas is sold. Occasionally, reinjection gas is augmented by gas or other hydrocarbons purchased from other operators. It is not customary to defer these purchase costs, although the injected hydrocarbons may have an inventory value to the extent that they will ultimately be sold. The reason advanced in support of charging the cost of these hydrocarbons to operations as they are purchased is that the cost should be matched against the revenue from the oil produced because of the pressurization.

Royalties (including net profit participations) and similar arrangements present no critical accounting problems when they represent a participation in current operations. Minimum royalties in excess of amounts due on production volumes and shut-in royalties are somewhat different. When these amounts are recoverable from future royalties they are usually, although not always, deferred. When they cannot be recovered from future royalties, however, they are universally charged to expense as incurred.

The production function in the mining industries is unique in that it involves the extraction rather than the creation of a product. Accordingly, the straightforward relationship of cost to market value of product found in most process-manufacturing operations is obscured. In many mining operations the value added by production costs is a minor part of total sales value. The mineral itself has a potential market value which production unlocks rather than creates; oil and gas are perhaps the best examples. In other mining industries, particularly nonferrous metals, production costs per unit may be substantial.

The existence of substantial potential market values poses the problem of determining the particular stage of the mining process at which to record inventories. In those extractive industries in which the mining processes of exploration, development, and production of one mining property are carried out simultaneously in a continuous flow, these functions tend to merge and introduce the additional complication of distinguishing one function from another.

These unique problems have been resolved in practice by:

1. Recognizing inventories for financial accounting purposes after the point of preliminary processing at the mine site; in some cases inventories of mined ore are ignored because they are relatively small and turn over very quickly. The elements of cost in inventory tend to be restricted to direct items.

2. Including with production costs some expenditures of an exploratory or developmental nature which are incurred subsequent to the beginning of commercial production.

RECOMMENDED ACCOUNTING PRACTICES

Selection of a Cost Center

Cost centers play an especially critical role in matching extractive expenditures with revenue from sale of minerals. The cost of the product in most manufacturing processes contains substantial amounts of material and labor which can be identified directly with specific units. Cost centers in these industries are required as a medium for collecting indirect costs and assigning them to units produced, but indirect costs are a minor portion of total product cost.

Much more substantial amounts are spent in extractive operations at a time when specific quantities of mineral reserves cannot be measured—and are not even known to exist. Prospecting, acquisition, and exploration expenditures are made to obtain mineral rights in an area or to obtain knowledge of the presence of minerals in an area, rather than to acquire specific known mineral reserves.

All expenditures, however, are directed toward the discovery and recovery of mineral reserves even though their presence is not known at the time. The mineral unit is the focus of extractive operations and the ultimate source of revenue. Costs must be appropriately identified with mineral units to achieve proper matching.

Although individual discovery and development costs are subject to depreciation and amortization, for example, lease and well equipment, shaft and tunnel development, timbering, roadways, other mining equipment, and related structures and facilities, their utility and useful life are intimately associated with the volume and extraction of underlying mineral reserves. They can be considered inventory costs associated with minerals-in-place as much as can the more direct acquisition and exploration costs subject to depletion.

Each mineral unit sold should bear an appropriate portion of discovery and development costs in order to obtain matching of effort and result. This is inventory accounting in a real sense. Minerals-in-place are a form of inventory, perhaps not as readily realizable, or measurable, as minerals already extracted but, nevertheless, inventory because they are already a product in the natural state. Often minerals-in-place are closer to a form ready for sale than raw materials carried in manufacturing inventories.

Cost centers are needed to attach discovery expenditures originally directed at areas of interest to the specific mineral units that will be sold. In line with the criteria mentioned in Chapter 3, a viable cost center should provide a consistent, objective, and logical result: consistent in producing a similar answer in similar circumstances; objective in being free of bias; and logical in the assumed effort/result relationship. As pointed out in Chapter 3, also, the choice of cost center affects not only the capital/expense decision but also the rate of amortization of capitalized or deferred costs.

Various cost centers might be used in extractive operations: acquisition units such as the lease or tract purchased; organizational units such as a territory, division or the company as a whole (full-cost concept); and operating units such as a mine, a petroleum reservoir, or other discrete mineral deposit.

Mineral Deposit Recommended as the Appropriate Cost Center. The first, and perhaps most important, recommendation to improve accounting practice in the extractive industries identifies the mineral deposit as the appropriate cost center.

> **Recommendation 1.** *The individual mineral deposit should be chosen as the cost center by which to identify costs with specific minerals-in-place.*

The recommendation states a broad principle which not only governs the capital/expense decision but also affects the definition of the total reserve quantity and the disposition of capitalized costs.

Mineral deposit as a cost center. The mineral deposit as a cost center goes directly to the cause-and-effect relationship of costs and revenue from specific mineral deposits. It limits this causal association of costs and minerals to those for which a direct link between effort and result can be identified. The mineral deposit provides a cost center which makes possible common application of capitalization and amortization policies consistent with the incidence of factors which give rise to the production of revenue regardless of the accidents of ownership or organizational structure. Therefore, it provides a cost center conducive to consistent definition by any company.

Mineral deposits are discrete units, each of which ultimately is the specific object of expenditures incurred to produce the minerals contained in that deposit. The presence of recoverable minerals in a specific deposit is justification for deferral of related discovery and development costs to the extent they are reasonably identifiable. The production of minerals from each deposit is the basis for matching amortization of deferred costs with revenue from sale of minerals. The exhaustion of recoverable reserves from a specific deposit signals the time at which all related costs should have been charged to expense.

The concept of the mineral deposit as the appropriate cost center should be applied with due regard for the unique character of each extractive industry. For example, a mineral deposit in the petroleum industry presumably would be an individually exploitable reservoir of hydrocarbons, but operating characteristics are frequently such that so literal a definition might result in very difficult practical accounting problems with corresponding limitations on the usefulness of the result. Hydrocarbon reservoirs are found in producing sands at various depths, each identifiable as a separate geological phenomenon and individually exploitable but none identifiable as the separate cause of particular components of related acquisition, exploration, and development costs. Acquisition costs are measured by surface acreage; discovery wells pierce all producing sands and production may be obtained simultaneously from all reservoirs through multiple completions in individual wells. Similarly, mining operations in other extractive industries can be carried out in several different ore beds from the same access facilities. The circumstances can create or compound a very difficult joint-cost problem.

To be practical, the concept of a mineral deposit as the most logical cost center should not be applied rigidly in circumstances such as those described above. The definition of property unit should be broadened to encompass more than one strictly defined mineral deposit, when a substantial amount of costs are incurred jointly on several deposits. The field, as used by petroleum companies to define a common operational unit, might be appropriate in the petroleum industry. The mine, as the property unit chosen in other industries, might include individually developed, separate ore bodies that together constitute one operating unit.

Cost centers based on acquisition units. Cost centers such as leases or other individual units of acquisition represent legal arrangements which reflect the accidents of ownership. A tract purchased or leased as one unit might contain several mineral deposits; it might also contain only part of a mineral deposit. To use the legal unit as a cost center would lead to the capitalization and amortization of costs in amounts and at rates that could vary according to the number of transactions by which the mineral deposit was acquired. If each transaction were regarded as a separate property unit, the relationship between deferred costs and minerals-in-place would be different than if the mineral deposit were regarded as the property unit. The sum of the several different depletion rates which would result from the "unit-of-transaction" approach would not be the same as the single depletion rate obtained by accounting for all costs related to that mineral deposit as a unit. An accounting practice capable of producing varying financial results in identical operating circumstances (volume of reserves, production rate, and deferred costs) is illogical and hinders comparability. The conditions for comparability and reasonableness of results are not present.

If all individually unsuccessful discovery and development expenditures are charged to expense (see Recommendation 5, page 72), cost centers based on acquisition units might give results not too different from cost centers based on mineral deposits. Although the rate for amortizing capitalized costs would be different, the amounts capitalized (only the successful in either case) would be the same. If, however, unsuccessful costs were capitalized in cost centers where production is obtained as the result of other expenditures, the difference in amortization rates between mineral deposit cost centers and acquisition unit cost centers could be quite marked.

Cost centers based on organization units. The "full-cost" concept of accounting for discovery and development costs is a result of defining the cost center in terms of an organizational unit—usually the company as a whole, but sometimes the entire domestic and the entire foreign operations as two cost centers. This concept confuses control centers with cost centers and does not create proper matching of effort and result.

Corporate activities are divided among organizational units (including divisions, production locations, functions, and so forth, as well as individual companies) primarily for more effective management control. Organizational units are centers of accountability in the sense of measuring performance against goals but not necessarily centers of accountability for establishing operating results on either a unit or corporate-wide basis. Organizational units are control centers, not cost centers.

The standards for measuring performance in any organizational unit may be many, for example, sales quotas, unit cost of production, share of market, degree of utilization of capacity, and so forth. In the extractive industries, standards of performance established for individual organizational units may be the number of successful versus unsuccessful wells drilled, tons of overburden moved or ore mined, the cost per foot of wells drilled, and so on. The point involved is that organizational units are designed for management control purposes rather than to obtain an appropriate matching of costs and revenue in accordance with a cause-and-effect relationship such as is required for financial reporting on the overall results of using corporate resources. This holds true even for those units such as the corporation as a whole or individual subsidiaries or divisions where top management performance is measured by net profit.

Responsibility does not of itself establish the cause-and-effect relationship required for appropriate matching. This is apparent in the illustrations above in which performance in an extractive company is measured by the number of successful versus unsuccessful wells, by the tons of overburden moved or ore mined or by the cost per foot of wells drilled. The distinction between a current expense charge and a capital charge is not important to measuring performance against this kind of standard. Even when performance is measured by net profit, responsibility does not establish a cause-and-effect relationship between expenditures and revenue. Organizational units are established to assign responsibility for optimum use of resources. They are not a means in themselves of measuring performance.

It is possible that an organizational unit may be an appropriate accounting cost center as well as a management control center; for example, the responsibility for a single mine or, in other industries, a single-process manufacturing plant. The relationship, however, is accidental and cannot be expected to occur consistently in all companies even though they may be operating under the same circumstances. The choice of organizational unit will vary depending upon management's philosophy of control, the numbers and quality of top and middle management people and other factors which are divorced from the cause-and-effect relationship between expenditures and revenue.

Proponents of "full-cost" accounting view unsuccessful expenditures as an inevitable part of the organizational process of finding and developing mineral reserves. They believe that more meaningful financial statements are produced by identifying all discovery and development expenditures with whatever reserves are discovered. Arthur Andersen & Co. supports this method as follows:

> ... the primary assets of an oil and gas producer are the underground hydrocarbon reserves—not the wells drilled to producing horizons. The cost of drilling dry holes and of other nonproductive exploration activities are a necessary part of the cost of discovering and developing the oil and gas reserves. There is no known way to avoid such costs. They should be capitalized since they are just as much a part of the cost of the reserves found as are the lease and well equipment on the producing wells.
>
> As a result of capitalizing all exploration and development costs, nonproductive as well as productive, the balance sheet will reflect the actual cost of the investment in mineral reserves, and not just that portion of the investment represented by successful ventures. Since management relates the total costs incurred to the mineral reserves found, the capitalization of all costs also provides more useful financial reporting for management decision-making.
>
> Furthermore, the amortization of the total costs on a pro-rata basis as the oil and gas reserves are produced results in a more meaningful income statement because of a better matching of costs with the related revenues. This treatment gives a better matching since it avoids the anomalous results sometimes encountered under present accounting practices, where, for example, a highly successful company may be reporting losses by charging a high portion of its investment in exploration activities to current operations, while an unsuccessful company may be showing attractive profits because it is depleting its mineral reserves without replacing them.[5]

In a research study of the Canadian Institute of Chartered Accountants, W. B. Coutts[6] also adopts the view that supports the "full-cost" concept but rejects the notion that the total reserves of a company should be treated as one property unit or cost center over which capitalized costs should be amortized. Coutts advocates that all preproduction costs be collected by areas of interest and amortized over the reserves in that area. If no reserves are found in the area, then the preproduction costs should be written off. "Area of interest" would coincide with project areas used by management in planning its operations.

---

[5] *Accounting for Oil and Gas Exploration Costs,* 1963, pp. 18-19.
[6] *Accounting Problems in the Oil and Gas Industry,* 1963.

Coutts believes the area-of-interest approach would avoid the incongruity inherent in a broad average derived from company operations as a whole—the assignment of identical costs to items which are not identical in nature. He recognizes that operations which are widespread geographically result in situations which may be so different in operating characteristics and in-place values as to make an overall average amortization rate meaningless for matching costs and revenue.

Full-cost accounting on a company-wide basis suffers from the defects of any broad average by disguising individual differences in a composite figure which represents none of the individual situations of which it is composed. Its proponents recognize the significance of this limitation by suggesting the possible need for separating domestic and foreign operations, but the suggestion merely segments the area of application without removing the limitations of broad averages.

Even on the area basis advocated by Coutts, which would reduce the objectionable effects of company-wide averages, the capitalization of both unsuccessful and successful expenditures in the area would tend to obscure comparison of the relative success of different companies in finding minerals. The practice submerges unproductive expenditures more than is warranted in view of the high risks.

The relatively unsuccessful company on a full-cost basis will tend to accumulate more capitalized costs in relation to the quantity of underlying minerals, and the additional cost will be worked out over the life of the mineral deposit through an increased unit amortization rate. Therefore, relatively poor performance will show up in a higher unit cost of minerals produced and sold. But this usually involves a long delay in recognizing relatively poor results. The investor needs timely information on results of company efforts, and the more current his knowledge of relative success the better informed he will be. Current disclosure of the loss from a relatively unsuccessful exploration program should be more significant to the investor than what would be conveyed only over the next 10 to 20 years by an increase in unit amortization rate if the losses were capitalized. Comparable or fair reporting can hardly result from an unsuccessful company showing much the same result currently as another company which was fortunate enough to have a very successful exploration program. That effect is created by capitalizing all costs of exploratory programs regardless of outcome under the full-cost concept.

If a common goal of company-wide operations was accepted as justification for averaging all costs and capitalizing unsuccessful expenditures, one could as well apply the method to costing in any industrial operation. For example, the carrying value of inventory might be the average of all costs applicable to a particular product line regardless of whether there was one or several plants engaged in manufacture of that product line or even some idle plants. Similarly, the costs of all research and development projects undertaken might be capitalized and added to the cost of one successful project, or all promotion costs could be capitalized and spread to products which become profitable—on the grounds that unsuccessful costs are inevitable in developing successful products. Neither of these practices is now acceptable. Deferring all expenditures because they have a common purpose, rather than through a direct identification of effort and result, gives too much weight to hope and insufficient weight to practical expectations.

The fact that under conventional accounting for finding and development costs one company might improve reported profits through curtailment of exploration expenditures and consumption of reserves is an accurate observation, but the cure for that does not require capitalization of all exploration costs. Appropriate disclosure of the total exploration commitment and movement in mineral reserves (as recommended in Chapter 8) would provide enlightenment without obscuring the relative success of the current program.

The consequences of a decision to adopt full-cost accounting are dramatic, as evidenced in recent years when changes have been made to full-cost accounting and accounts reported for prior years have been restated. Reported losses may be turned into restated profits, and although the resulting increase in resources and net worth presumably is more than adequately supported by estimated realizable market value of mineral reserves underground, the implications of reporting profits when current revenue is not sufficient to sustain both production and immediately unsuccessful exploration costs should not be ignored. In a sense, a company in this position is not yet a going concern; it differs in future investment prospects from the more mature company which can bear the inescapable, continuing unsuccessful costs of maintaining its reserves out of current income. The investor ought to be made aware of this difference in circumstances, and full-cost accounting tends to obscure it.

Admittedly, it is hard to draw clean-cut lines between the successful and unsuccessful costs of finding and developing mineral reserves, but the relative proportions of each are important operating differences between companies and should be reported in the way most likely to disclose the differences on a timely basis. Full-cost accounting will not accomplish that result. The requirement for demonstration of a reasonably direct cause-and-effect relationship between costs that are deferred on the one hand and economically recoverable mineral reserves on the other will accomplish the purpose.

There is no direct causal relationship between capitalized expenditures associated with discovery and development of one discrete mineral deposit and revenue obtained from sale of minerals from another discrete deposit. Consequently, the natural relationship of cause and effect by which consistent and comparable financial reporting can be obtained would be destroyed under full-cost accounting.

Allowing the Medium or the Nature of an Expenditure to Affect the Capital/Expense Decision

Some companies capitalize certain contracted exploration, development, and outside legal costs related to acquisition of properties or productive exploration and development efforts, but charge similar costs incurred by their own staff to operations. Some companies continue to charge the intangible portion of development costs to income as incurred even though these costs are identifiable with specific mineral reserves for which tangible development costs are capitalized.

Costs should be capitalized when they are directly associated with minerals to be produced and sold in the future. The basic criterion is result of the effort, rather than operating methods or nature of the cost.

A distinction between own-staff and contract costs may be justified when company staff is used to provide continuing supervision, administration, and maintenance of operations and occasional unusually large efforts are performed by contract. In that case, the outside contract costs are a direct incremental cost for an identifiable individual effort which, if productive, should be deferred or capitalized.

An analogy is found in industrial companies which follow incremental costing for administration and supervision involved in constructing their own plant facilities. Only contract expenditures are capitalized—not any portion of the costs associated with the time of their own engineers. But even under this policy, direct costs of construction by a company's employees are customarily capitalized. Also, if a company's own engineers are engaged in substantial, continuing capital construction activities, as in most public utilities, appropriate amounts of recurring administrative and supervisory costs are allocated to construction accounts.

The governing guideline is that expenditures which benefit future operations should be capitalized. There is no basis in theory for applying this guideline differently solely because the method of expenditure is different. Neither is there justification for recording in the balance sheet of a going concern only the tangible portion of development costs. The relationship of cost to minerals-in-place which are expected to be produced and sold in the future is the overriding consideration. Method and nature of payment are not significant.

Based on the foregoing analysis, the second recommendation of this study emerges.

> **Recommendation 2.** *Neither the medium of expenditure (company's own force vs. contract) nor the nature of the expenditure (intangible vs. tangible) should affect the amount of cost otherwise properly associated with minerals-in-place and capitalized.*

The general adoption of this recommendation would eliminate inconsistent practices in applying what should be the governing guideline in identifying costs to be deferred and matched against future revenue.

Transactions Occurring During the Prospecting and Acquisition Phases

Substantial expenditures prior to exploration of specific properties, in the form of geological and geophysical costs and considerations paid for acquisition of property rights, are made in the hope that mineral reserves in commercially recoverable quantity finally will be found. Most of these expenditures, however, will never lead directly to the production of minerals.

Although some of these preexploration expenditures may be made steadily (geological and geophysical) and others intermittently (the price of acquiring property rights), they share a common characteristic of being spent at a time when they cannot be identified with specific mineral reserves. The presence of minerals will not be determined until actual exploration is carried out. In the meantime, the only identifiable results of these preliminary expenditures are an increase in general knowledge of possible mineral sources and the acquisition of title to any minerals that may be found.

The objective of reporting these expenditures should be to write off those that are unsuccessful and to capitalize those that will ultimately be identifiable as part of the cost of specific mineral reserves from which future revenue will be obtained.

Since preexploration expenditures are made without knowing whether any mineral discoveries will ever result, it is unrealistic to pursue any accounting policy which would tend to produce a result inconsistent with the fact that the major part can never be identifiable with specific mineral deposits. Accordingly, policies for deferral and disposition of costs incurred in the preexploration stage of operations should result finally in capitalizing that portion of cost which ultimately proves to be directly associated with specific deposits of economically recoverable minerals. Conversely, policies should result in charging to operations, in the periods which establish the probability of loss, that portion of cost which will never be directly identifiable with specific mineral deposits.

Geological, geophysical, and other prospecting costs represent the continuing costs of the general search for areas likely to contain minerals and may appropriately be charged to expense immediately. This type of prospecting is an essential fixed cost of exploration activity. It may be compared with research costs directed at general objectives rather than specific projects. These prospecting costs are remote from the discovery of specific mineral deposits. The effort produces at best only a favorable prospect for acquisition and more intensive exploratory effort.

On the other hand, an argument might be made that geological and geophysical costs which lead directly to the acquisition of property rights should be deferred. As a practical matter, improvement in financial reporting would not necessarily follow. In many, if not most cases, appropriate portions of the total geological and geophysical cost typically incurred in broad areas cannot easily be identified with specific properties acquired. Even when the identification problem might be solved, the amounts finally associated with successful projects would be substantially reduced if the recommendation to amortize costs of undeveloped properties made later in this study is followed.

In retrospect, it would have been appropriate to capitalize some of these costs related to properties which proved to be productive. To that extent, the capitalized cost of producing properties will be understated. Unless some extraordinary conditions exist, the understatement is not likely to be material. Charging all geological and geophysical costs to income as they are incurred does not appear to be too high a price to pay to reflect the substantial risks involved in preliminary exploration operations.

The immediate result of geological and geophysical expenditures is a decision to acquire or not to acquire rights to unproven mineral prospects. Whether the ultimate result of expenditures made to acquire unproven mineral rights will prove to have value in recoverable reserves will not be known for some time. Despite that difference in time lag between expenditure and result, both geological and geophysical expenditures and acquisition cost expenditures are essentially exploratory in nature. Although it may take several years to determine whether the cost of acquiring specific mineral rights is an asset or a loss, experience indicates that most acquisitions will be abandoned. When a property right of several years' duration is abandoned, its acquisition cost is seen in retrospect as a part of past costs of the continuing program of prospecting and preliminary exploration during the years necessary to establish the fact of loss.

The considerations paid for property rights are proven ultimately to consist of two parts: the minor part which can be identified with commercially recoverable reserves is an asset; the major part which cannot be identified with commercially recoverable reserves is a loss. If we accept the view that the loss finally determined is a cost of exploration, then, in retrospect, it was an element of prepaid exploration expense contained in the acquisition cost. The expected loss portion of acquisition cost, properly deferrable in the first instance, should therefore be amortized on a systematic and rational basis over the periods during which the property is held for exploration (see Chapter 5).

The elements of acquisition cost properly deferred until ultimate disposition by write-off or capitalization should include expenditures directly related to the acquisition or retention of title. For example, lease bonuses, the purchase price of properties bought in fee, brokers' commissions, special outside legal counsel fees, lease extension payments, and advance royalties which are not avoidable by termination of the lease are properly deferrable because they relate directly to the acquisition of title.

Indirect expenditures supporting acquisition activity, such as legal and administrative staff costs, including land and lease department activities and delay rentals, are more appropriately charged off currently as a continuing cost of sustaining the preliminary exploration activity.

Other elements in the category of "carrying costs," such as shut-in royalties and minimum or advance royalties recoverable from future production, are part of the cost of successful properties. Shut-in royalties are a cost of foregoing current revenue in hopes of more favorable conditions in the future. Although it might be argued that these payments should be capitalized since any benefit relates to the future sale of minerals, the hoped-for advantage is speculative. Accordingly, shut-in royalties should be charged to expense as incurred.

Minimum or advance royalties on producing properties which are recoverable from future production should be charged to operations currently unless there is strong assurance that future production will be sufficient to recover the excess cost. Accounting for these items must be based on the best estimate of the extent to which they are a realizable asset.

The analysis of transactions occurring prior to identifying the presence of specific mineral reserves leads to two recommendations:

> **Recommendation 3.** *Expenditures for prospecting costs, indirect acquisition costs, and most carrying costs should be charged to expense when incurred as a part of the current cost of exploration.*
>
> **Recommendation 4.** *Direct acquisition costs of unproven properties should be capitalized and the estimated loss portion should be amortized to expense on a systematic and rational basis as part of the current cost of exploration.*

The intent of these recommendations is to charge to expense in the period which establishes the fact of loss those expenditures which will ultimately not be directly identifiable with specific mineral deposits. The recommendations, if followed, would restrict the deferral of these preliminary exploration costs to the direct acquisition costs of property rights, and would require amortization of the expected loss portion of those deferred acquisition costs.

Accounting for Transactions During the Period of Identification and Development of Mineral Reserves

The initial degree of uncertainty as to the presence of minerals in a property unit lessens as exploration and development operations intensify. The uncertainty eventually becomes one of measurement rather than of existence. Expenditures are directed at particular targets and can be associated directly with specific property units and mineral deposits.

To the extent that these expenditures can be associated with specific mineral deposits in commercial quantities, they should be capitalized and eventually amortized as the minerals are produced and sold. The accounting problems consist of identifying the elements of cost properly deferrable and selecting the appropriate basis for amortization.

It would be possible to regard all expenditures related to the mineral deposit as part of the unit cost of minerals found. Thus, all exploration costs of a capital nature on prospects which prove to be commercial successes would be capitalized even though some of the particular expenditures might not, by themselves, result in the discovery of commercially recoverable mineral reserves. Similarly, all development costs of a capital nature would be capitalized as costs of specific mineral deposits. Unproductive core and well drilling on defined mineral deposits which have commercially recoverable reserves would be illustrations of the unsuccessful expenditures in question. The results would be analogous to deferring normal spoilage costs in a manufacturing process or to those obtained under the full-cost concept except on a more restricted scale.

Although a few petroleum companies capitalize the cost of development dry holes, most companies in the extractive industries (except for full-cost companies) expense those costs which by themselves are unsuccessful even though the costs may be incurred in areas where mineral deposits are known to exist.

In extractive industries other than petroleum and natural gas there has been a tendency to charge to expense during the production phase successful expenditures which would have been capitalized during the development phase. (However, extensive costs of a development nature which obviously prepare for several years' production are commonly deferred even though the mine is in the production phase.)

In allocating expenditures to the periods benefited, the phase of mine operations is a useful guide in determining whether expenditures are primarily for future or current production—whether they should be capitalized and amortized over the periods benefited or expensed as incurred. The characteristics by which development and production phases can be distinguished are fairly well established in accounting literature and the income tax law.

The income tax regulations provide the following useful definition of the point at which the exploration phase ends and the development phase begins: "... after such time when ... deposits of ore or other mineral are shown to exist in sufficient quantity and quality to reasonably justify commercial exploitation by the taxpayer" (IRS Reg. 1.616-1(a)).

The point at which the development phase ends and production begins is defined by Maurice E. Peloubet:

In general, the development stage is completed when the principal activity becomes commercial production. It frequently happens that commercial minerals are extracted incidentally to development work, but so long as the prime purpose of the operation is development, incidental production of commercial minerals is merely a credit to the cost of development rather than operating income.[7]

In general, successful development costs of a new ore body should be deferred, but development costs to extend an already developed ore body should be expensed except when they are so extensive as to make several years' production accessible. Often several ore bodies are made the target of development expenditures from common access facilities, for example, several levels may be developed from one access shaft. If the expenditures at one level prove unproductive and the facilities are abandoned because commercial production is not foreseeable, the expenditures should be charged to operations. In that case no identifiable benefit accrues to ore bodies at other levels which may become commercially producible.

Costs should be carried forward when it can be demonstrated that they benefit future operations. That is the essence of the matching concept. When individual exploration and development efforts fail to find minerals by themselves, the benefit to future operations can be established only indirectly through assumption of some added benefit to reserves elsewhere in the relevant property unit. The burden of supporting that assumption is not necessarily the same for both exploration and development expenditures. Each development expenditure is directed at outlining or preparing for production specific mineral deposits, whereas the target of exploration expenditures is more general. (However, "development" effort sometimes ranges far from the initial strike and may take on the characteristics of an exploration activity.)

As a practical matter, it would be difficult to maintain a distinction between unsuccessful development and unsuccessful exploration costs for accounting purposes. A reasonable period for amortization of unsuccessful development expenditures cannot be determined except in those cases in which the entire mineral reserve is developed before production begins and the type of facility provided by the expenditure would have benefited production for the life of the entire mineral deposit. The petroleum industry tends to this type of development, but in other industries where mining occurs in successive stages de-

---

[7] "Accounting for the Extractive Industries," *Economics of the Mineral Industries,* 1964, p. 407.

velopment is scheduled to benefit only that portion of total reserves needed for relatively imminent production. In the latter case, unsuccessful development expenditures cannot be attributed to the reserve as a whole but, at best, can only be attributed to a portion of the reserve estimated on the basis of some hypothetical conclusion as to the number of years' production that would have benefited by an equivalent successful expenditure.

The capitalization of unsuccessful expenditures on producing property units would have little effect were they but a minor and relatively constant proportion of total expenditures. They are, however, a major part of expenditures and the success ratio varies among companies and properties. That fact alone could cause considerable cost variances in the exploration and development of mineral deposits. The possibility of significant variation in success is increased by the suggested definition of the cost center. In Recommendation 1, the cost center is not limited to a single mineral deposit occurring in a self-contained producing sand or ore bed, but is broadened to include the possibility of several such deposits occurring in a fairly well defined common geological structure constituting an operational unit.

If all exploration and development costs associated with a producing mineral deposit were capitalized regardless of the results achieved, an important difference in results of operations could be disguised by deferral of costs not directly related to future revenue. That same consideration, which was discussed in connection with the full-cost concept, is valid also in determining the appropriate disposition of unsuccessful expenditures on producing mineral deposits. The critical question is whether the investor is better served by being informed of adverse results of unsuccessful expenditures in the period in which they occur or in subsequent periods. The conclusion is that the investor is better served by being informed of adverse results in the period in which they become evident.

This discussion of expenditures during the period of identification and development of mineral reserves leads to the fifth recommendation of this study.

> **Recommendation 5.** *Unsuccessful exploration and development expenditures should be charged to operations even though incurred on property units where commercially recoverable reserves exist.*

This discussion excludes from unsuccessful exploration expenditures amounts which lead to the discovery of commercially recoverable reserves if the related facilities are abandoned and the deposit is developed by other means. For example, offshore drilling for petroleum or natural gas may occasionally result in a discovery well that is abandoned in favor of locating the platform for subsequent development drilling in a more advantageous position in relation to the total property. The cost of the abandoned well is appropriately a part of capitalized successful development costs since it was a successful expenditure in its own right.

Accounting for Hydrocarbons Purchased for Injection

The cost of gas or other hydrocarbons purchased for injection in oil or condensate reservoirs bears aspects of both current production cost and of inventory cost. The circumstances are similar in effect to the joint-product/by-product situation in which the relative significance of revenue from the secondary product determines the allocation of costs. If the revenue from the secondary product is significant in relation to total revenue, costs are allocated between the joint products. If the revenue from the secondary product is not significant in relation to total revenue, the secondary product is treated as a by-product and all costs may be allocated to the primary product.

Hydrocarbons are primarily injected to promote recovery of liquids. The cost therefore can be viewed as a current production expense attributable to creation of revenue from the sale of those liquids ("by-product" concept). This view is strengthened to the extent that recovery and sale of the injected hydrocarbons, after they have completed their role in promoting recovery of liquids, is doubtful or not measurable. Furthermore, injected hydrocarbons, such as gas, commingle with native hydrocarbons in the reservoir and are not separately distinguishable if and when finally produced.

On the other hand, it is sometimes fairly certain that the injected hydrocarbons will be recovered and sold after all liquids have been recovered. In these circumstances, the cost becomes a factor attributable in part to the revenue which will be created at that future date. If the revenue from the sale of the injected hydrocarbons is expected to be significant, the cost should properly be carried forward to be matched against that revenue ("joint-product" concept).

Usually, neither the purchase cost of injected hydrocarbons nor the revenue from their sale, once their primary role is complete, is sufficiently material in relation to other costs and revenue to warrant deferral of the cost. Furthermore, the practical problems of uncertainty in measurement of the base of mineral reserves over which to amortize the cost, caused by commingling with native hydrocarbons, and the possible uncertainty of recovery of volumes injected, may affect the quality of estimate of recoveries to such an extent that deferral of purchase cost is unwarranted.

If, however, the volumes recoverable are reasonably ascertainable and the amounts of either related cost or related revenue are material in relation to other operating factors, the inventory aspects of the purchase cost—its direct relationship to expected revenue from sale of the injected volumes—cannot be ignored.

This study recommends:

> **Recommendation 6.** *The cost of gas and other hydrocarbons purchased to repressurize reservoirs should be recorded as an expense of the periods which receive the most benefit. Ordinarily, the cost should be charged to the period of reinjecting the hydrocarbons, but if a measurable and significant amount of revenue is expected to result from the sale of the reinjected hydrocarbons, the cost should be deferred and matched with that revenue. In the latter situation, appropriate provision should be made for any loss because of nonrecoverability of a portion of the volumes injected.*

Mine Restoration Costs

The undertaking to restore or improve property upon completion of mining operations is an unavoidable cost of producing minerals. If matching is to be obtained, revenue should bear a ratable portion of these costs. A reasonable exception would be for property restored substantially concurrently with production, e.g., strip-mining operations when overburden from the next development acreage is used to restore the acreage just mined.

Failure to record substantial accumulations of restoration costs to which the mining company is committed by its operations understates current expense and overstates expense of some future period when restoration must be made. Thus, the recommended practice in accounting for mine restoration cost is:

> **Recommendation 7.** *The estimated cost of restoring mined properties should be accrued ratably as minerals are produced.*

Summary of Recommendations Regarding the Capital/Expense Decision

In the survey of practice regarding the capital/expense decision and the analysis of the problem, several recommendations have been developed. The first, which identifies the mineral deposit as the appropriate cost center, is a broad recommendation with general application. The second recommendation rejects practices which allow the medium of payment or the nature of an expenditure to affect the capital/expense decision. The others recommend accounting practices for individual types of transactions. These include accounting for transactions occurring during the prospecting and acquisition phases, transactions during the period of identification and development of mineral reserves, purchases of hydrocarbons for injection, and mine restoration costs. Adoption of all these recommendations as general practice in making the capital/expense decision would significantly improve accounting in the extractive industries and narrow the areas of difference.

5

Disposition of Capitalized Costs

SURVEY OF PRESENT PRACTICES

The mining process gives rise to two general types of costs deferred to future operations: those which relate to properties not fully tested for minerals by exploration, and those which relate to proven mineral reserves that are partially or fully developed. Balance sheets of mining enterprises reflect these assets in categories such as: "undeveloped or unproven leaseholds"; "nonproducing mine properties"; "producing leaseholds"; "mines and mining rights"; "lease and well equipment"; "land"; "buildings and equipment"; "deferred development costs"; and "preliminary development and preoperating expenses."

Capitalized costs of equipment and facilities with a determinable physical life less than that of the mining operations in which their values will be consumed present the same accounting problems as capital assets in other industries. Physical deterioration measured by time or output of units produced is the measure of exhaustion of useful life and consequently the basis for disposition of capitalized costs. Movable equipment and buildings used in mining operations are capital assets of this type and are accounted for in this manner.

The disposition of other capitalized costs which relate to potential or proven minerals-in-place is a much more difficult accounting problem. It begins with the definition of property units by which to identify capitalized costs and continues through the selection and measurement of mineral units in reserve and those extracted. The circumstances permit a variety of answers.

Accounting for the Disposition of Undeveloped Property Costs

Substantial expenditures are made to acquire exploration and mineral rights. The basic acquisition unit in the petroleum industry is a lease or concession, or several leases covering an area of interest — all of which contain provisions for landowners' royalties on oil or gas found and produced. In other extractive industries the basic acquisition unit is a tract of surface and mineral lands or occasionally mineral lands only, more commonly purchased in fee and sometimes accompanied by a commitment to pay continuing royalties on any minerals produced. The right to minerals in a particular reservoir or ore body may consist of several leases or purchases, or a particular lease or purchase may cover more than one separate deposit of minerals. Since most unproven mineral prospects never become productive, accounting for the disposition of undeveloped property costs is a special problem in the extractive industries.

Undeveloped property costs are transferred to producing property accounts or charged to operations, depending on the results of exploration or the sale of undeveloped property rights. Many companies systematically amortize unproven property costs to income during the periods that the properties are held for exploration.

Most companies in the extractive industries, taken as a whole, make no adjustment to the carrying amounts of undeveloped property rights until the presence or absence of commercially exploitable reserves has been determined. On this basis, costs applicable to undeveloped properties are charged to operations when the decision is made to abandon them and to producing property accounts when commercial quantities of minerals are found. When very large acreage holdings are explored in stages over a period of time, the disposition of total cost may be gradual, since an appropriate part of total cost may be allocated to each area of the total held as it is proved. The allocation is usually made on the basis of surface acreage. If both surface and mineral rights are owned in fee, the usual practice is to assign a nominal cost to surface land when the disposition of cost is made. In some industries, sand and gravel for instance, land containing potential mineral deposits may be purchased at farmland prices and may retain a value as farmland at least equal to cost even though the mineral reserves are not developed. In that situation, no portion of the property cost is written off until the land is sold.

In the petroleum industry, many companies, possibly a majority, amortize undeveloped property costs prior to proving the property, either as a general practice or as to those individual properties with unusually high acquisition costs, such as offshore leases and foreign concessions. Amortization may be selective, at rates based on experience, or a proration over the lease term. A few companies maintain an amortization reserve at 50% of property costs, in recognition of the fact that the amortization charge is not deductible for tax purposes. Some of the other companies amortize on a net-of-tax basis, but most ignore the potential tax deductibility feature.

The API survey of industry practices showed that most of the companies surveyed amortized undeveloped property costs.[1] These findings are shown in Table 1, opposite.

Professor Brock's study [2] made eight years earlier showed that only 13 of 61 companies amortized leasehold costs. Ten of the 13 were among the largest 26 companies and only 3 were among the smallest 35.

Interestingly enough, in view of the preceding statistics, only 4 of the 110 annual reports of petroleum companies analyzed in Chapter 8 disclose a practice of amortizing undeveloped leasehold costs. None of the other mining industry reports makes any reference to disposition of undeveloped property costs.

Advocates of the practice of amortizing undeveloped property costs contend that the very high incidence of nonproductivity justifies a conservative practice. Amortization also tends to smooth out the impact on results of operations of irregular charges for abandoned property costs which are frequently significant. Advocates of the practice of nonamortization support their view by arguing that passage of time alone does not reduce the value of investment in undeveloped property and that proof of loss in value should be obtained before writing off the investment.

When undeveloped properties are proven to be productive after their acquisition costs have been partially or wholly amortized, some companies transfer both cost and related amortization reserve to producing properties, but others transfer only the cost and adjust the reserve through income, as necessary, to maintain a reasonable reserve balance in relation to the remaining undeveloped property costs.

---

[1] *Report of Certain Petroleum Industry Accounting Practices,* 1965, p. 27.
[2] Horace R. Brock, "Petroleum Accounting," *The Journal of Accountancy,* December 1956, p. 63.

TABLE 1

**Amortization of Undeveloped Property Costs
by Selected Petroleum Companies**

Method	Frequency*
Amortize:	
At rates based on experience	9
On a selective basis	4
Over terms of the leases	3
Down to a percentage of capitalized costs	3
Over life of producing properties	1
Total which amortize	20
Do not amortize; charge to expense when relinquished	11
Total reported	31

* Three companies indicate more than one practice.

Accounting for the Disposition of Producing Property and Equipment Costs

Capitalized mine and equipment (other than movable equipment) costs are usually amortized as the mineral reserves are produced. Costs are ordinarily amortized on a unit-of-production basis but may occasionally be amortized by equal annual charges to operations over the period during which the reserves are expected to be produced. In some cases, notably nonferrous metal producers, the cost of mining rights is not amortized at all or is amortized on an arbitrary basis over a period of years determined by management's judgment.

The sale of a fractional interest in producing properties poses accounting questions similar to those in the sale of undeveloped properties (discussed in Chapter 6). Both cost recovery and allocation of cost to sales methods are in common use, with a slightly greater preference for allocation of cost than is the case with sales of undeveloped interests (see Chapter 6, Table 5, page 103).

Although all capitalized producing property costs (other than the nominal amounts charged to surface land) are quite generally considered to be properly amortizable against revenue, several companies in the nonferrous metal industry do not amortize the acquisition costs of mines and mining rights. Others amortize by equal charges over a period of years without regard for the rate of depletion of mineral reserves.

The review of annual reports to stockholders of 61 nonferrous mining companies discussed in Chapter 8 revealed 27[3] which either definitely or probably do not record depletion on producing property costs. None of the other 204 companies in other mining industries included in the review revealed whether property costs are depleted.

Kennecott Copper Corporation adopted a policy of recording depletion on producing property costs in 1967. Prior to that year the following explanation was included in its annual reports:

> *Mining Properties:*
>
> Over the years the ore reserves have increased as a result of development work and improvements in methods of recovery of metals which make possible the treatment of lower grades of ore. Accordingly, no provisions for depletion have been considered necessary.

Phelps Dodge Corporation records depletion on metal mines on a unit-of-production basis but with a cautionary note of explanation disclaiming any representation that the charge is an accurate measure of depletion actually sustained.

Magma Copper Company reported applying a 20% rate as a general policy to the remaining unamortized cost, less salvage value, of all property, plant and equipment at the beginning of each year, but reported amortizing the development cost of one large mine over a 20-year period.

The practice of not recording depletion on acquisition costs of nonferrous metal mines reflects doubt concerning the possibility of obtaining a realistic unit-of-production rate in view of the problems in estimating total mineral reserves in hard-rock underground mines. Many companies believe that recording no depletion is less susceptible to misinterpretation, as long as reserves are still in sight, than is recording inaccurate depletion. Nevertheless, nonferrous mining companies are more likely to report mineral reserve quantities in annual reports to stockholders than the other seven groups of mining companies reviewed in Chapter 8.

Effect of the Cost Center and Mineral Reserve Base on the Disposition of Capitalized Costs

The rate of amortization of capitalized property, development, and equipment costs is affected significantly by the choice of cost centers and the selection of reserve units and methods of measurement. These

---

[3] Subsequently reduced to 25 by changes in accounting policy in 1967 by The Anaconda Company and by Kennecott Copper Corporation.

choices have an obvious direct effect on unit-of-production depletion, depreciation, and amortization; and they have a potential limiting effect on time depreciation should the estimated reserves not be sufficient to outlive depreciable equipment and facilities.

As an illustration, the petroleum industry commonly uses the lease as its basic accounting unit and cost center. Costs are collected by lease, and those which are capitalized are written off over the production from reserves estimated to be recoverable from that lease. Several leases of various sizes may be held on a particular reservoir and the costs of drilling and equipping each are not likely to be the same; neither are the reserves underlying each likely to be the same. Nevertheless, each lease may be tapping the same producing sand and pool. Since costs and production to reserve ratios of these leases cannot be expected to be proportionate, the sum of the depreciation and amortization charges on each of the leases would obviously be different from what it might be were the pool as a whole considered to be the property unit and all lease costs depleted over the aggregate reserve.

To extend the illustration, those few petroleum companies which have recently adopted the so-called full-cost concept view the enterprise as a whole as one accounting unit and losses from some individual efforts as an inevitable part of the cost of the few successful efforts. Since unproductive costs cannot be related directly to specific reserves, under the full-cost concept they must be accounted for as part of the cost of the overall reserves of the enterprise. Even if the effect of capitalized individual losses is ignored, the amortization of total costs on the basis of total reserves results in a different charge to income for depletion, depreciation, and amortization than would amortization based on individual leases because the relationship of cost to underlying reserves and to production rates is altered.

Selection of the depletable mineral unit and its measure also influences the rate of amortization of capitalized costs. Joint products are common in the mining industry. They are joint products in the classical sense: no one mineral can be produced without the others. In these circumstances, are the reserves for depletion purposes to be estimated on the basis of the principal product or on the basis of a composite of all products? The choice is unimportant where each unit extracted contains the same proportions of joint minerals, but it is important where the proportions change; for example, where gas and oil are produced together and the gas is reinjected for pressure maintenance to be produced again and sold after the oil has been exhausted.

A more important discretionary reserve estimate factor is the measure of the reserves: developed, proved, or probable.

To these complicating factors must be added the natural difficulties of making accurate estimates of mineral reserves. The resources cannot be fully defined in many situations and fluctuate in terms of what is economically recoverable in response to changes in market demand and technological advances.

Cost Center. Most petroleum companies use lease, block, or concession as the basic property accounting unit and cost center. Other mining industries favor individual mine or tract, the latter being more common in surface mining industries such as sand and gravel. About one-third of the petroleum companies in the API survey, however, use district, division or region, field or pool. One nonferrous metal producer uses the company as a whole to account for property costs, but most of them use individual mines.

Only 31 of the 265 annual reports reviewed in Chapter 8 disclosed the property accounting unit used (see Table 2, opposite). Responses to the API survey on the selection of the property accounting unit [4] were as follows:

Operating Unit	Frequency of Use
Leases, concession, or block	19
District, division, or region	5
Field or pool	5
Company-wide	3
Not answered	1

The mineral deposit is recommended as the appropriate cost center (see Recommendation 1, Chapter 4). Units such as lease, block, or concession are contractual units in which various persons have interests of different kinds and degree, whereas individual mines are natural geological units. The preponderant use of contractual units for property accounting in the petroleum industry is probably a result of obligations to account for operations to other parties at interest rather than an acceptance of contractual units as logical or natural units for cost center purposes. When lands and mineral rights are held in fee, as is common in mining industries other than petroleum, the need for accounting to other persons with ownership rights is not present. In these industries each mineral deposit is viewed as a separate natural unit for property accounting.

---

[4] *Report of Certain Petroleum Industry Accounting Practices,* 1965, p. 30.

TABLE 2

Property Accounting Units Disclosed in 265 Annual Reports

Primary Activity	Area	Company-wide	Lease	Mine
Integrated petroleum	1	6(b)		
Nonintegrated petroleum	3(a)	9(b)	3	
Nonferrous metal		1		7
Bauxite, asbestos, and uranium				1

(a) Includes one full-cost concept company.
(b) Includes 6 integrated and 6 nonintegrated petroleum producers which have adopted the full-cost concept.

Mineral Reserve Base. Both proved and developed reserves are used as a depletion base to amortize capitalized property costs. These terms may have different connotations in the various mining industries. For discussion purposes, proved reserves are defined to include those reserves which are estimated to be recoverable with additional development expenditures and developed reserves are defined to include only those reserves which can be produced with existing facilities.

Companies which develop substantially all the mining property in advance of the major part of production, as is common in the petroleum industry, favor developed reserves as the depletion base. Other companies which engage in successive development operations as production advances lean toward proved reserves. A few petroleum companies also use proved reserves to amortize capitalized development costs, and reflect in the unit rate of amortization estimated additional future costs to be incurred in developing the total reserves. Some petroleum companies use proved reserves to deplete leasehold costs, and developed reserves to depreciate or amortize tangible and intangible drilling costs.

In some surface mining operations for nonmetallic minerals, depletion and amortization are computed in the ratio of surface acres mined to total surface acreage in the tract.

Of the 26 companies responding to the API survey query on reserve base, 20 used developed reserves and 6 used proved reserves. Three of these companies used proved reserves for leasehold costs and developed reserves for tangible and intangible drilling costs.

None of the 265 annual reports reviewed in Chapter 8 disclosed the reserve basis, although 42 of them stated that depletion was based on unit-of-production methods.

Substantially all companies periodically revise reserve estimates and make appropriate adjustments to unit-of-production rates. The change is made prospectively, not retroactively. It must be emphasized that even the most careful and objective estimate of recoverable reserves contains a wide margin for error. Not only are there limitations on the reliability of physical measuring techniques, especially in extensively faulted underground structures, but the commercial feasibility of recovering reserves will be influenced by future changes in mining and conversion technology, market prices, and production costs. Considering the relatively long periods of recovery for most mineral deposits, significant changes in these factors, and consequently in the estimate of commercially recoverable reserves, become a virtual certainty.

The reserve base and depletion rate are influenced also by the extent to which joint products are taken into consideration. Most petroleum companies deplete on the major product base but some combine both gas and oil in reserve estimates. The predominant conversion factor is relative sales value of gas and liquids. One company in the API survey reported using British thermal unit (Btu) content as a common denominator.

In other mining industries unit-of-production rates are usually based on the major product. When products are combined for this purpose, both weight and relative sales value are used as common denominators.

Summary of Present Practices

The abandonment, sale, or production of mineral properties requires appropriate accounting for capitalized acquisition, exploration, and development costs. Some of these costs relate to capital items of a depreciable nature, such as movable equipment and structures, where either the disposition of the item itself or the passage of time is the natural measure of exhaustion as in any other industry. The bulk of capitalized costs in the mining industries, however, is related to mineral reserves, either directly as in the case of acquisition and exploration costs or indirectly as in the case of development costs applied to the production of reserves.

Accounting for the disposition of capitalized costs related to mineral properties requires a choice of property unit and, if production from the unit is forthcoming, of reserve base and reserve unit.

Although a few companies have adopted a company-wide property accounting unit, the great majority uses units of lesser size, consisting of contractual units, such as leases or concessions which require accounting to other parties at interest, or natural units, such as a particular mineral deposit held in fee.

Capitalized costs of undeveloped properties which prove to be nonproductive are charged to operations at a time no later than the abandonment of the property and, in a significant number of cases, ratably over a period of years prior to proving the property. The latter treatment recognizes the fact that most ventures prove to be unsuccessful. Amortization of acquisition cost is more common when the acquisition cost is high or the acreage covered is large and proof of reserves by exploration progresses in successive stages. Companies that follow the full-cost concept never record abandonment losses—unless, of course, they go out of business.

Either proved or developed reserves are used as a base to calculate relative exhaustion of mineral reserves and related acquisition costs of producing properties. Although developed reserves are ordinarily used for amortization of development costs, a few companies use proved reserves and reflect in the amortization rate additional future development costs. Some companies use proved reserves for acquisition costs and developed reserves for development costs. Other companies, notably nonferrous metal mines, either do not deplete property acquisition costs or base a depletion rate on judgment rather than the rate of exhaustion of reserve units.

The choice of reserve unit is no problem if only a single product exists, but in many mining operations joint products are recovered. In these circumstances, a decision must be made whether to measure production on the basis of the major product or on the basis of an aggregation of all products. In the petroleum industry, the major product is most commonly used. There is, however, a somewhat greater tendency to reflect in the reserve base gas produced from wells classified as oil wells than liquids produced from wells classified as gas wells. The common denominator used to aggregate reserve units is usually relative sales value of the products.

In other mining industries the reserve unit is either the major product or joint products aggregated on the basis of weight. In any given industry in which production of joint products occurs in constant proportions, as in most mining industries other than petroleum, the alternative of a single major product or aggregated joint products produces the same rate of depletion or amortization of capitalized costs.

Mineral properties may be sold in place, either in whole or in part. If the entire property accounting unit is sold, no unique accounting problem arises; but if part of an interest in the property is sold, a decision must be made whether to treat the proceeds as income or as a reduction of cost. Practice is mixed.

RECOMMENDED ACCOUNTING PRACTICES

Accounting for That Portion of Deferred Acquisition Costs Representing Prepaid Exploration Cost

As indicated in Chapter 4, only a minor portion of acquisition costs can be identified ultimately with commercially recoverable mineral reserves. The major portion of capitalized acquisition costs will probably never be directly identified with minerals-in-place and represents, therefore, an element of prepaid exploration cost. These deferred costs should be charged ratably to the periods during which the property is held for exploration on the basis of a systematic and rational amortization method. Accordingly, this study recommends:

> **Recommendation 8.** *The current cost of exploration charged to expense should include a charge for the amortization of that portion of acquisition costs which will probably never be directly identified with minerals-in-place.*

Either time or rate of progress of exploration activity may be the more appropriate basis on which to establish an amortization rate. The choice depends upon circumstances such as the expected retention period and the rate of exploration.

A fixed period of time, during which exploration must be completed, as under a mineral lease, provides a satisfactory basis for amortization. If, however, there are definite plans to complete exploration of the property before the lease expires, a shorter period of amortization based on the expected progress of exploratory activities would be more appropriate.

The cost of properties held in fee requires a more selective approach, since a fixed time period during which exploration must be carried out is not available. Average experience regarding periods of retention and exploration, whether company- or industry-wide, might provide the most satisfactory basis for amortization of the capitalized cost of both leased and fee properties when the properties are substantially homogeneous. In those industries, sand and gravel for example, in which properties are purchased in fee for their prospective mineral content at prices which are not inconsistent with alternative uses of the property, such as for farming or ranching, the alternative resale or use values should be considered in determining the extent of probable loss subject to amortization.

If average experience factors are applied to amortization of a group of property costs, costs of abandoned properties should be charged against the accumulated amortization charges and no gain or loss should be shown. The cost of properties which prove to be successful should be transferred to producing property accounts at the gross cost. These recommendations are consistent with the concept of average experience as applied in other situations, such as group depreciation accounting.

An extraordinarily large concession or acquisition may create a property so unique in the company's experience as to make group accounting based on average experience inappropriate. Each such unique property should be accounted for separately. If the property is leased, the primary lease period provides a systematic and objective time base for amortization, unless the rate of exploration progresses more rapidly than the passage of time. If it is expected that the property will be fully explored before the lease expires, costs should be amortized or transferred to producing properties ratably with the progress of exploration measured in acreage. This "progress" method is also appropriate for large individual properties owned in fee.

The accumulated provision for loss on a separately accountable unique property which proves to be productive should be transferred to the producing property account as an offset to the gross cost of property and should not be reversed by a credit to income. Reversal of amounts previously charged to operations would be inconsistent with the basis for amortization. The basis rests on the view that probable loss represents a prepaid exploration expense to be charged ratably to the periods during which the property is held for exploration and that exploration costs charged off as incurred should not be retroactively capitalized, even if eventually identifiable with properties which are later found to contain mineral reserves.

Most publicly held companies probably have a sufficient number of individual undeveloped property units to provide a satisfactory basis for the application of group accounting for probable loss even when the number includes large individual property units.

Accounting for the Disposition of Capitalized Costs Associated with Minerals-in-Place

If the capitalization of expenditures is limited to those which are directly identifiable with specific mineral deposits, it follows that amortization should be related to extraction of those mineral reserves with which the costs have been identified. Depending on the nature of the expenditure, capitalized costs may be amortized ratably with the volume of production or depreciated on a service life basis.

Elements of tangible property, such as some structures and equipment which have useful lives shorter than that of the mineral deposit, should be depreciated on an estimated service life basis. Although not necessarily different in character from similar tangible property in other industries in which time is ordinarily the basis for measuring the rate of expiration of useful life, these expenditures may be more highly specialized to one purpose—the production of minerals. Accordingly, if the wear and tear of production is the primary cause of service life exhaustion, the depreciation rate is more appropriately based on the rate of production of total units expected to be serviced. If, on the other hand, the passage of time is the more important element of service life exhaustion, time should be the basis for depreciation.

Thus, as a corollary to the initial recommendation which was introduced in Chapter 4 and which identifies the mineral deposit as the appropriate cost center in the extractive industries, this study further recommends accounting for the disposition of capitalized costs associated with minerals-in-place as follows:

> **Recommendation 9.** *Capitalized costs associated with minerals-in-place should be amortized ratably as the related minerals are extracted but may be amortized on the basis of time when time is the controlling factor in consumption of economic usefulness.*

Three decisions are involved in determining the appropriate rate for amortizing deferred costs identified with mineral reserves: (1) definition of the total reserve quantity benefited, (2) allocation of total costs among joint-product minerals, and (3) selection of the appropriate stage in the extractive operations to measure exhaustion of capitalized cost.

Definition of Total Reserve Quantity Benefited. The identification of particular costs with minerals-in-place which are expected to produce future revenue requires that they be deferred to the periods when the minerals are produced and sold. The assumption of future benefit which requires the capitalization of current expenditures is justified only to the extent that these costs contribute to revenue which might reasonably be expected at some time in the future. Unquestionably, costs deferred on the assumption of future benefit should be amortized to expense as revenue from the sale of the related minerals is realized. The primary difficulty appears to be identifying the particular quantity of minerals-in-place benefited by deferred or capitalized costs.

In general, acquisition and discovery costs deferred should be identified with the total reserves expected to be produced from the property unit being used as a cost center. Development costs deferred should be identified with that quantity of reserves made available for production. These deferred development costs might relate to the total recoverable reserves in the property unit or some lesser part, depending on the methods used to develop the mineral deposits.

In industries, such as petroleum, in which development facilities are used for substantially the entire life of the mineral reserves in the property unit, the basis for amortization would approximate the total recoverable reserves, as nearly as they can be estimated. More development cost would be deferred in those circumstances than in industries such as metal mining in which development tends to be scheduled to maintain rather than to increase production. For the most part, costs in these industries are more akin to production than to development costs. Unusually extensive development expenditures which relate to more of the reserve body than that to be mined within the next year or so are properly capitalized and amortized over expected production from the developed area.

The recommended accounting in each of these situations conforms to the rationale of the matching principle: development costs should be related to the number of mineral units made available through the expenditures.

Some companies use an amortization rate based on total expected development costs and total expected minerals to be produced, rather than actual expenditures to date and related developed reserves. This variation is acceptable because it conforms to the basic principle of matching costs with revenue from reserves benefited. It would, of course, be an error to relate actual development costs to total estimated minerals-in-place if a significant quantity is not yet developed, for that would depart from the concept of identification of particular expenditures with specific reserves.

Allocation of Total Cost to Joint-Product Minerals. The theory of costing joint products is a subject of recurring fascination. Accountants, economists, and even lawyers have grappled time and again with the problem of dividing joint costs in a manner which would result in a meaningful separate cost for each joint product. The absence of success is not due to lack of effort or ingenuity but to the impossibility of the act.[5]

By definition, true joint products are locked together inseparably by their nature or the manner of their production so that one cannot be produced without the other; instead both must be produced, initially at least, to obtain either. The most clear-cut examples are various combinations of minerals contained in the same ores. Petroleum and natural gas are also true joint products even though gas can be separated at the surface and sold in that form or returned to the reservoir formation.

Most companies identify capitalized costs of mineral deposits with the principal mineral and amortize the costs as that mineral is extracted. Some companies combine the major minerals by a common denominator and relate capitalized costs to the aggregate. Common denominators used are relative sales value or some shared physical characteristic such as weight, or, in the case of energy fuel, Btu content.

If all minerals but one are clearly by-products, amortization of capitalized costs in accordance with the rate of production of the major product is appropriate. The circumstances that pertain to joint-product mineral deposits differ from those that relate to primary/by-product mineral deposits. Since each joint-product mineral is significant in itself, the combined costs must relate in some measure to each joint-product mineral. Ideally, an appropriate portion of total capitalized costs should be amortized as each of the joint products is produced and sold. In fact, there is no way of doing this that is demonstrably correct. The essence of the joint-cost situation is that the cause-and-effect relationship between expenditure and revenue can be identified only in total.

In many cases amortization of capitalized costs at the rate of produc-

---

[5] An excellent, comprehensive study is contained in the N.A.C.A. Research Series No. 31, *Costing Joint Products*, 1957.

tion of the predominant joint product might be satisfactory because approximately the same result would be accomplished as an allocation of capitalized costs among all joint products. For example, when a deposit contains two minerals in a common ore as joint products occurring in approximately constant proportions, amortization of capitalized costs in relation to extraction of either mineral would yield the same result as amortization of an allocated cost to each of the mineral products.

If one mineral were produced prior to the other, however, amortization of all costs on the basis of the earlier production alone would be unreasonable since there would be no remaining cost to be matched against the revenue from the mineral produced later. A common illustration is that of natural gas associated with crude oil or with condensates in petroleum reservoirs where the gas produced is reinjected to aid further production of the liquid hydrocarbons and is sold only after liquids are recovered.

Accordingly, it is recommended that amortization of deferred costs identifiable with mineral reserves be based on an aggregation of joint-product mineral reserves. The common denominator used to amortize capitalized costs should avoid a disproportionate burden of cost on any one product. Common physical characteristics such as weight, Btu content, or volume are the natural denominators for aggregating mineral reserves. They can, however, yield individual product cost allocations which have little meaning in relationship to realizable sales price of the products. The resulting matching of costs with revenue has correspondingly limited meaning.

In the terms of reference in this discussion, the assignment of capitalized costs between joint mineral products by using relative market prices of the products appears to be about as reasonable a method as can be devised in the circumstances. By recognizing ability to absorb cost, the relative market price method avoids carrying forward an allocation of costs disproportionate to expected revenue. To that extent, the method results in a reasonable matching of costs and revenue.

Little more can be said for the method. The resulting amortization charge is not a reliable product cost; joint products can have no individually determinable costs prior to the point of separation in the production process. Furthermore, relative sales prices do not of themselves determine costs. Their use results only in an assignment of indivisible joint costs on a basis which avoids retention of capitalized joint costs disproportionate to the revenue to be expected from remaining minerals. Because of these limitations, frequent changes in the common factor should not be made simply to conform to minor fluctuations in relative market prices of the joint products.

Selection of Appropriate Stage in Extractive Operations to Measure Exhaustion of Capitalized Costs. Depletion and amortization of capitalized costs related to mineral reserves on the unit-of-production basis are recorded by some companies at the time of production and by other companies at the time of sale. Production usually is measured when the mineral has been brought above ground and is ready for shipment from the mine site. Crude oil in field tanks, crushed and screened stone in the quarry, and ore ready for transfer to the smelter are considered to be produced; broken ore in a mine or quarry is not.

Whether production or sale is the more appropriate point at which to record amortization of capitalized mining costs depends on whether inventories of minerals produced but not yet sold or transferred to subsequent refining operations are reported as assets. If inventories are reported as assets, then depletion, depreciation, and amortization charges based on the number of units of mineral reserves produced should be recorded as an element of inventory cost.

In most operations, no significant accumulation of extracted minerals occurs at the mine site and separate inventory values are not recorded in financial statements. In other operations, minerals may be extracted and stockpiled deliberately in excess of current sale or current processing demands. If stockpiled inventories are material and realization through sale is probable, they should be recorded in the financial statements and the carrying amount should include a proportionate share of capitalized and deferred mining costs by recording depletion, depreciation, and amortization at the time of production.

Depletion of Nonferrous Metal Mines. Many companies in the nonferrous metal industry, and a few in other industries, record no depletion of the acquisition costs related to mining properties and claims. The same companies, however, amortize capitalized expenditures for mining structures, equipment, and development work over useful lives measured by physical depreciation or exhaustion of mineral reserves benefited by the expenditures. This distinction between acquisition costs and subsequent facilities is said to be based on the difficulties of obtaining reliable estimates of total recoverable mineral reserves. Location and measurement of ore bodies and veins is extremely difficult and the borderline between uneconomical and economical quantities of minerals can shift significantly during the relatively long production periods typical of these mining operations.

In terms of ultimate reserves produced, these acquisition costs are usually insignificant as can be dramatically illustrated by mines which have produced for scores and even hundreds of years. On the other hand, development and production costs are substantial and limit the amount that can economically be paid for the mineral rights. These circumstances are distinguishable from those in the petroleum industry in which production costs tend to be less significant than acquisition costs.

In the face of the several conditions which limit the ability to arrive at a meaningful unit of depletion rate, it is often held that depletion charges are subject to misinterpretation because they imply a more precise rate of exhaustion of mineral reserves than is justified by the facts.

From a conceptual viewpoint, the direct association of these property costs with mineral reserves, which was the basis for capitalization, requires that they be charged to income ratably over the periods during which the minerals are produced. Difficulty of measurement is not usually considered sufficient justification for failure to charge income with the cost of benefits which are consumed by operations. A best estimate of appropriate depletion rate with accompanying explanation of its limitations would provide a reasonable balance between theory and practicality and a better answer to this difficult question than no depletion at all. The total supply may be exceedingly difficult to measure but it is not inexhaustible. Some portion of the deferred property cost should attach to each unit of minerals-in-place as it is extracted.

In view of the difficulties of estimating what quantity of minerals might ultimately be produced from a property unit, it could be argued that deferred costs related to the entire mineral reserves should be amortized by equal charges over a selected number of years without regard to actual production rates. This expedient, however, does violence to the identification of particular costs with specific reserves whenever the rate of production is erratic, even as would be the case when deferred costs are held intact without any amortization. The justification for deferral of these costs is the existence of mineral reserves; there is no approach to amortization more logical than estimate of total mineral reserves with which those costs are identified and application of the derived rate to current production.

6

Accounting for Revenue, Special Conveyances, and Joint Operations

The ability to convey rights to minerals-in-place which have not yet been produced gives rise to many unusual contractual arrangements and difficult accounting problems. In some cases the conveyance is limited to the mineral reserve equivalent of a specified dollar amount; in other cases the conveyance consists of a continuing interest in production or net profits. The accounting problems involve the timing of reporting revenue and related costs.

In addition to having these unique financial reporting situations, companies in the extractive industries frequently participate in joint operations for exploration, development, and production activities. These activities are sufficiently extensive to require consideration of the manner in which they should be reported to investors.

SURVEY OF PRESENT PRACTICES

Production Payments

A common source of revenue is the sale of a portion of minerals-in-place for cash, known as a "carved-out production payment." The seller is obligated to pay all production costs, but has no obligation to complete the payment if recoverable reserves prove insufficient.

Nearly all companies defer recognition of the sales proceeds as revenue until the minerals are produced. The API survey of petroleum companies reports that three-fourths of the companies which record these sales as deferred income reduce the deferral by the amount of income tax applicable to the sale (for tax purposes, production payment proceeds are taxable in the year of sale).[1] A small minority of companies records proceeds as sales in the year received and accrues estimated future lifting costs; the future tax effect of production costs deducted when incurred is sometimes but not always reflected in the accrual. The principal reason given for the majority practice is the difficulty of definitely and objectively determining income prior to the time actual lifting costs are known. The only company in the API survey which reports that it follows the minority practice of not deferring proceeds states that it relies on the fact that the payment is a completed sale at the time of the transaction with no further obligation other than to lift the production-payment oil, an obligation which can be reflected by accruing estimated lifting costs.

The review of 265 mining company stockholder reports which are discussed in Chapter 8 suggests that general practice in all extractive industries is to defer recognizing revenue from sale of carved-out production payments. As shown in Table 1, page 96, 53 companies reported sales of production payments, all of which were recorded as deferred revenue with one exception: minor amounts from the sale of oil payments by a coal producer were recognized as revenue at the time of sale although recognition of revenue from sales of coal payments was deferred.

The API survey obtained definite results through specific questions of respondents. The results obtained from the review of annual reports are less conclusive because they depend on the degree and quality of disclosure. There is no way of being certain that the 212 companies not reporting production payments in their annual reports did not, in fact, sell production payments or record them as income when sold. Although the balance sheet of a company which sold production payments and reflected the proceeds in income should reflect a liability for estimated future lifting costs, this liability would not necessarily be disclosed separately. However, since the review disclosed only one incidental exception to the reported practice of deferral, the conclu-

---

[1] The API survey, however, was made prior to the effective date of *APB Opinion 11*, "Accounting for Income Taxes," which held that the "net of tax" form of presentation should not be used for financial reporting.

TABLE 1
Frequency of Disclosure of Production Payments in Annual Reports to Stockholders

	Total Number in Group	Number Reporting Production Payments
Integrated petroleum	54	11
Nonintegrated petroleum	56	20
Iron	25	2
Nonferrous metal	61	2
Coal	18	5
Bauxite, asbestos, and uranium	10	None
Salt, sulfur, and potash	8	2
Cement, stone, gravel, and sand	33	11
	265	53

sion must be that deferral of proceeds from sales of carved-out mineral production payments is the dominant practice. It was not clear from this review whether an income tax effect is commonly attributed to these payments and correspondingly deferred. Most companies in the API survey provide deferred income taxes for the effect of sales of carved-out production payments.

In summary, most companies apparently recognize revenue from sales of a portion of minerals-in-place over the periods during which the minerals are produced; a smaller number of companies apparently recognizes the entire proceeds as revenue when the sale is made.

ABC Transactions

Mineral reserves are frequently acquired by purchase of proven properties in an "ABC" transaction. The initials refer to the three parties involved: seller, purchaser, and financier, in that order. Perhaps the easiest way to explain an ABC transaction is by an example, based on somewhat exaggerated assumptions to emphasize financial reporting implications.

Assume that A has found and developed an oil reserve containing an estimated 32,000,000 barrels which he wants to sell in a capital gains transaction, and that B is interested in acquiring A's working interest with a minimum immediate cash outlay in the manner that will permit the maximum reduction of income tax allowed by law. The objectives of A and B can be achieved if B purchases A's interest for, say, $10,400,000 in cash, subject to a production payment of $15,000,000, at an appropriate interest rate, to be satisfied out of 75% of future production and A sells the retained production payment to a third party, C, for the face amount.

When these transactions are consummated: (1) the seller, A, will have received $25,400,000 in cash, any gain on which is taxable at capital gains rates; (2) the financier, C, will hold an economic interest in $15,000,000 worth of oil which will be produced over, say, five years, and will receive a satisfactory annual rate of interest on the unpaid balance; and (3) the purchaser, B, will own the working interest in the property subject to C's economic interest in sufficient oil to satisfy the retained payment, say, 6,000,000 barrels, for which B must pay the production costs.

Note that B will have paid in cash considerably less than the present value of the reserves. More importantly, the balance of the consideration will be satisfied out of pretax rather than after tax dollars. For tax purposes, B will record only the cash paid, $10,400,000, as the cost of the properties (apportioning it between lease and well equipment and leasehold cost in an equitable manner).[2] The portion of revenue from future sales of oil dedicated to the oil payment, 75%, will be excluded from B's gross income (and included in C's). All the production costs, including those attributable to the 75% dedicated to the oil payment, are borne by and are deductible by B.

For financial accounting purposes, the seller and the financier, A and C, have no unusual problems. The buyer of the property, B, has to answer these questions:

> What is the appropriate cost of the properties—
> Cash only?
> Cash and cost of producing the oil payment reserves?
> Cash and value of oil payment reserves?

---

[2] An exception is made when the portion of production not reserved to the minerals payment is insufficient to cover the production costs and that event could have been foreseen from the terms of the sales contract at the time it was drawn. In that case, any excess of production cost over revenue would have to be capitalized for tax purposes and would become subject to depletion.

What revenue should be reported during the payout period—
All sales, including the oil payment portion?
Only B's portion?

How should production costs applicable to oil payments be recorded—
Charge to expense as incurred?
Accrue estimated costs as part of property cost and amortize over working interest production?
Defer costs as incurred and amortize over working interest production?

In practice, three methods of accounting for the purchase of mineral rights subject to a reserved minerals payment have been developed:

1. The cash portion only is capitalized and is amortized on the basis of net production (excess of working-interest share over production-payment share); all production costs are charged to expense as incurred.

2. The cash portion is capitalized and a percentage of production costs equal to the production payment percentage is capitalized as incurred, sometimes net of income tax effect; a variation is to capitalize estimated future lifting costs of the production payment at the time of purchase with credit to a liability account. The capitalized costs are amortized on the basis of net production.

3. The entire consideration, both cash and face value of the production payment, is recorded as an asset with a corresponding liability for the production payment; the capitalized cost is amortized on the basis of gross production and all production costs are charged to expense as incurred.

Although total net income over the life of the property is the same under each of the three methods, net income for individual years varies considerably depending on which of the three methods is used. A comparison of these effects can be prepared from the data previously assumed, adding the assumptions of a level annual rate of production of 1,600,000 barrels (a 20-year life for the field), cash lifting costs of $800,000 a year, and a 50/50 split of the $10,400,000 cash consideration between depreciable equipment and depletable leasehold cost (see

CHAPTER 6: ACCOUNTING FOR REVENUE, SPECIAL CONVEYANCES, AND JOINT OPERATIONS

Tables 2, 3, and 4). Interest, production taxes, and interperiod allocation of income tax effects under *APB Opinion 11* (see Chapter 7) are ignored in these examples.

The alternative beginning balance sheets will contain the items shown in Table 2, page 100. Net income for the first year would be reported as indicated in Table 3, page 100, and that pattern would be repeated during each of the five years assumed to be the payout period. In the sixth and subsequent years, net income would be reported as shown in Table 4, page 101.

ABC transactions are more prevalent in the petroleum industry although they are beginning to spread to other mining companies. The petroleum industry is split between accounting methods 1 and 2; each method is used by 12 companies in the API survey. Only one company in that survey used method 3.

Proponents of method 1, capitalization of only cash payments, argue that since the buyer obtains no economic interest in the oil or gas required to satisfy the production payment and has no liability for the payment other than from production, capitalizing either the lifting costs or the face value of the mineral payment would be misleading. Other considerations are that method 1 is more conservative in the sense that it defers more income to later periods than do methods 2 and 3 and it is the method required for income tax reporting.

Proponents of method 2 argue that the cost of the mineral interest includes the commitment to lift the oil to satisfy the production payment and that to charge this portion off currently understates the asset cost and unreasonably burdens operations during the years of lifting the production payment and correspondingly lightens the burden in subsequent years. In effect, they hold that the costs to lift the production payment are additional payments on an installment purchase.

The sole exponent of method 3 in the API survey views the production payment as a lien against minerals-in-place from which a liability, the face amount of the payment, is to be satisfied.

The buyer of a producing property must also apportion the consideration between the mineral reserves and equipment or other mining facilities. Other than statements that apportionment is made on an "equitable" basis, the source materials which were used for this study do not provide information on actual practice. From a tax viewpoint, it is desirable to allocate as much as possible to depreciable property and as little as possible to depletable leasehold or mine costs, since depletable costs will be recovered only to the extent that they exceed percentage depletion.

TABLE 2

Beginning Balance Sheet Items under Alternative Methods of Accounting for Mineral Rights Purchased in an ABC Transaction

	Method 1	Method 2	Method 3
Producing leasehold	$5,200,000	$8,200,000	$20,200,000
Lease and well equipment	5,200,000	5,200,000	5,200,000
Accrued estimated lifting costs attributable to oil payment (50¢ a barrel)	—	3,000,000	—
Liability for oil payment	—	—	15,000,000

TABLE 3

Net Income in Periods Prior to Payout under Alternative Methods of Accounting for Mineral Rights Purchased in an ABC Transaction

	Method 1	Method 2	Method 3
Gross revenue (@ $2.50 a barrel)	$1,000,000	$1,000,000	$4,000,000
Lifting cost	800,000	200,000	800,000
Depletion (cost)	80,000	126,160	1,010,000
Depreciation	80,000	80,000	260,000
Income tax	20,000	20,000	20,000
	980,000	426,160	2,090,000
Net income	$20,000	$573,840	$1,910,000

Note: Both depletion and depreciation are on a unit-of-production basis using the following reserves:

Methods 1 and 2: gross reserves less estimated portion dedicated to oil payment = 26,000,000 barrels

Method 3: gross reserves = 32,000,000 barrels

Conveyances of Fractional Interests in Undeveloped Mineral Properties

The conveyance for cash of fractional interests in undeveloped mineral properties gives rise to a question of whether the transaction should be treated as (1) a sale of assets, requiring an appropriate

TABLE 4

Net Income in Periods Subsequent to Payout under Alternative Methods of Accounting for Mineral Rights Purchased in an ABC Transaction

	Method 1	Method 2	Method 3
Gross revenue (@ $2.50 a barrel)	$4,000,000	$4,000,000	$4,000,000
Lifting cost	800,000	800,000	800,000
Depletion (cost)	320,000	504,613	1,010,000
Depreciation	320,000	320,000	260,000
Income tax	890,000	890,000	890,000
	2,330,000	2,514,613	2,960,000
Net income	$1,670,000	$1,485,387	$1,040,000

allocation of property cost between the interest conveyed and the interest retained and a recognition of gain or loss, or (2) as a recovery-of-cost transaction, requiring that the total proceeds be credited against the property costs allocable to both the interest conveyed and the interest retained. Proceeds from a conveyance may be pledged for development of the property in which the fractional interest is conveyed. This arrangement complicates the accounting question since it raises the further question of whether the transaction is a cost-sharing agreement. Further complications are added by the fact that the interest conveyed may be either working, nonoperating, or fractions of both.

Although majority practice is split rather evenly between cost recovery and sale methods, some preference for the sale method is shown when a fractional working interest alone is sold. A few companies credit proceeds to income with no corresponding charge for a portion of cost, especially when the entire working interest is conveyed and an overriding royalty is retained.

The use of cost recovery rather than the sale and allocation of cost method is founded on conservatism, in response to the speculative nature of the investment, and the difficulties of arriving at a reasonable allocation of cost.

When the proceeds from transfer of a part interest (either a fractional working interest or a continuing nonoperating interest) are pledged for development of the property, about two-thirds of the companies credit them to property costs, usually prorated among leasehold, equipment, and intangible costs. Income is recognized under this method only if proceeds should exceed *total* costs. The other companies credit proceeds first to property costs and then to income to the extent they exceed the part of costs allocable to the interest conveyed; this method does not recognize a loss when proceeds are less than the cost allocable to the interest conveyed.

Table 5, opposite, shows the incidence of practice in accounting for sales of interests in both undeveloped and producing oil and gas leases except those involving a carved-out production payment or sharing arrangement. It summarizes the responses of the 32 petroleum companies that participated in the API survey. (The sale of producing leases is discussed in Chapter 5.)

Joint Operations

Mining companies frequently engage in joint activities ranging from fractional interests in specific properties to jointly owned affiliated companies. Joint operations on a large scale are particularly common in foreign ventures, and income from these sources is often substantial. When investments in joint operations are direct, the owner's fractional interests in properties, income, and expense are accounted for in its statements as transactions occur. When an investment in joint operations is made through a jointly owned corporation, the common practice is to carry the investment at cost and to record income as dividends are received. The annual reports reviewed in Chapter 8 reveal that a few companies have adopted equity accounting for jointly owned companies.

RECOMMENDED ACCOUNTING PRACTICES

Production Payments

A few companies recognize revenue from the sale of carved-out production payments in the year in which the sale is made, but most companies report the revenue proportionately as the related minerals are produced. In the former case, provision for future production costs,

TABLE 5

Sales of Fractional Interests in Oil and Gas Leases

1. Working interest conveyed with a nonoperating interest retained.

   Three transactions are involved as follows:

   Interest conveyed: Working interest
   Interest retained:
   a. Production payment
   b. Continuing, nonoperating interest
   c. Continuing, nonoperating interest and a production payment

2. Fractional working interest conveyed with a fractional working interest or a fractional working interest and a nonoperating interest retained.

   Four transactions are involved as follows:

   Interest conveyed: Fractional working interest
   Interest retained:
   a. Fractional working interest
   b. Fractional working interest and a production payment (out of the interest conveyed)
   c. Fractional working interest and a continuing, nonoperating interest (out of the interest conveyed)
   d. Fractional working interest; continuing, nonoperating interest (out of the interest conveyed); and a production payment (out of the interest conveyed)

3. Continuing, nonoperating interest conveyed with a working interest retained.

4. Working interest in a specified depth in an undeveloped lease conveyed with working interest in other depths retained.

	Undeveloped Lease			Producing Lease	
Transaction	Allocate Cost	Reduce Cost by Proceeds	Record Proceeds as Income	Allocate Cost	Reduce Cost by Proceeds
	(Number of Companies)				
1 a	7	7	—	7	8
1 b	6	8	6	13	10
1 c	4	6	3	11	4
2 a	12	7	1	15	2
2 b	6	4	—	6	3
2 c	7	5	3	9	5
2 d	5	3	3	6	4
3	6	3	1	6	3
4	7	11	1	—	—

Source: American Petroleum Institute, *Report of Certain Petroleum Industry Accounting Practices*, 1965, pp. 50-51.

if material, is made in the year of sale; in the latter case, production costs fall naturally in the same period as revenue is recognized.

Under the deferred-revenue concept, a secondary consideration must be appropriate classification of the credit in the balance sheet. A split by industry is apparent at present: the petroleum industry generally treats the proceeds as a noncurrent deferred credit, whereas other industries classify the proceeds as a current liability.

The differences of opinion regarding timing of revenue and classification of proceeds are not surprising in view of the complicated characteristics of a carved-out production payment transaction.

Timing of Revenue. From a legal standpoint the facts involved in the sale of a carved-out minerals payment suggest that the proceeds be recorded as revenue in the period of sale, because title to the minerals passes and proceeds are received at the time the contract is executed. Although the minerals are still in place, the seller's obligation to produce them in satisfaction of the minerals payment can be measured and recorded as a liability by estimating related future production costs. This treatment of revenue is required for tax purposes (although the related costs of production cannot be deducted until they are incurred).

Recording revenue from minerals payments in the period of sale has a parallel in reporting sales of warehouse goods not yet delivered by the seller but to which title has passed because they have been sequestered from other inventories and identified as property of the buyer. This basis of reporting revenue is theoretically sound but not commonly used. One authority states:

> From a legal standpoint the sale is completed by the passing of title, and accountants acknowledge the importance of this criterion. Title passing, however, is a highly technical matter and a convenient procedure for booking revenue from day-to-day is usually employed without stressing legal niceties. The act of invoicing, together with actual delivery or consignment to a common carrier, provides the most popular and suitable occasion. Sales for future production and consignment sales should not be reported as income.[3]

As indicated in the passage quoted above, there has been general reluctance in all industries to accept the reporting of revenue until

---

[3] Paul Grady, *Accounting Research Study No. 7*, "Inventory of Generally Accepted Accounting Principles for Business Enterprises," 1965, p. 76.

substantially all conditions attached to the sale have been met by the seller. Under this realization convention delivery is generally held to be an act of performance necessary to justify recording revenue. This requirement of the realization convention is sometimes modified when it would otherwise produce an unreasonable result but not when production consists of a relatively uniform flow of small units.

Consideration should also be given to fairness of reporting revenue from sale of minerals in excess of a sustainable rate of production. A production payment sale does not necessarily represent a sustainable increase in production and sales. It is an advance sale of minerals that would otherwise have been sold in future periods. In that respect, the transaction resembles a contract for sale more than it does a contract of sale.

The following recommendation conforms to the realization convention and provides the best balance of the considerations set forth above:

Recommendation 10. *Sales of a limited, partial interest in minerals-in-place (carved-out production payments) should be recorded as revenue in the periods during which the minerals are produced.*

Classification of Deferred Proceeds. A current liability classification for deferred proceeds from sales of carved-out production payments is consistent with the view, held by some, that these transactions are a financing medium and the proceeds are, in effect, a loan to be repaid from next year's production. The choice of a current liability classification is also supported by some on the grounds that at least part of the proceeds will be required to satisfy the seller's obligation of bearing the out-of-pocket costs of producing minerals to satisfy payment. The merits of this view become more apparent as the relationship of out-of-pocket production costs to proceeds increases in significance. This may explain the tendency in those extractive industries with relatively large production costs to classify deferred proceeds among current liabilities.

A deferred credit classification, on the other hand, is consistent with the concept of an advance sale of minerals not yet produced. It is incongruous to classify as a liability proceeds which are to be recorded as sales in future periods; no accounting convention supports the conversion of liabilities to revenue. Unearned revenue might justifiably be classified among current liabilities when the assets sold are included in inventories. The discovery value of mineral resources, from which production payments must be satisfied, is not recorded in the accounts; the capitalized discovery and development costs are typically unrelated to the discovery value of the mineral resources and are classified as noncurrent assets in financial statements.

Therefore, it is recommended that:

> **Recommendation 11.** *The deferred portion of proceeds from sales of carved-out production payments should be classified as noncurrent unearned revenue.*

Sales Subject to Contingencies

The realization convention requires that revenue must be earned as well as received. Consequently, sales transactions contingent upon future events cannot justifiably be recorded as revenue unless the uncertainty represented by the contingency is likely to be removed.

Amounts collected under take-or-pay contracts in excess of amounts due for actual deliveries and amounts collected under temporary contractual gas prices are properly reported as revenue only to the extent that the present contingencies can be expected to be removed by future events. In either situation, the probability of the contingency becoming effective must be assessed and revenue recorded or not recorded as appropriate. Either decision requires footnote disclosure of any material amount subject to contingencies.

Under take-or-pay contracts the seller has a contingent obligation to deliver additional product in the future, if demanded by the purchaser, without additional payment. Although the obligation to deliver product is similar to that under a carved-out production payment, it differs in that it is not a fixed obligation. Unlike the carved-out production payment, take-or-pay contracts require future delivery only to the extent demanded by the customer. Usually customers can be expected to take delivery but sometimes circumstances might indicate that event to be unlikely (for example, a foreseeable shortage of refining capacity or demand during the "grace" period). The following recommendation reflects these probabilities:

> **Recommendation 12.** *Amounts collected under take-or-pay contracts in excess of current deliveries should be recorded as unearned revenue unless circumstances indicate that the purchaser will not take delivery in future periods.*

In contrast with take-or-pay contracts, evaluating the contingent obligation to refund a portion of the amount collected under temporary contractual gas prices is more difficult, because the contingency depends on the extent to which the contracted prices will be approved by the regulatory authority. Regulatory actions are not as easily predicted as is a purchaser's intent to take a quantity of additional product for which he has already paid. Nonetheless, significant amounts collected under temporary contractual prices that are likely to be refunded should not be reported as revenue when collected. Despite the difficulty, it is frequently possible to determine the extent to which temporary price increases are likely to be approved, particularly under the area approach to establishing gas prices now favored by the Federal Power Commission. Under the area approach, patterns of allowed prices develop so that it is possible to predict, with a reasonable degree of certainty, the likelihood of approval of contracted price increases and to determine the amount that should be reported as revenue at the time funds are collected.

Thus, the following recommendation for reporting amounts collected under temporary contractual gas prices is essentially the same as the foregoing recommendation for reporting amounts collected under take-or-pay contracts. Each recommendation requires assessment of probabilities of future events.

Recommendation 13. *Amounts collected under temporary contractual gas prices subject to refund should be recorded as revenue of the current period only to the extent that refund is unlikely.*

Determining the Cost of Mineral Rights Acquired by Special Conveyances

Acquisition costs of mineral rights acquired by special conveyances require particular attention, since the consideration generally includes commitments other than or in addition to the commitment to pay cash. The cost convention, discussed in Chapter 3, recognizes that obligations assumed as well as cash paid are properly a part of the cost of assets acquired. In this section, attention is given to the problem of identifying the elements of cost in specific kinds of acquisition transactions in which rights to minerals-in-place are acquired wholly or partially in exchange for commitments other than a commitment to pay cash. Three types of transactions are involved: ABC transactions, farm-outs, and carried interests. The following recommendation is developed:

> **Recommendation 14.** *The capitalized acquisition costs associated with minerals-in-place should include the cost of commitments as well as the amount of cash paid outright. In ABC transactions, the estimated production costs rather than the face amount of the retained mineral payment should be included.*

Purchaser. In each of the three types of transactions discussed, the purchase of mineral rights involves an agreement to develop or produce a portion of the minerals-in-place to which the seller retains title. The seller's retained interest may be fixed in amount, as is the principal in an ABC transaction, or it may be a continuing interest, either working or nonworking, as in a farm-out or carried-interest arrangement. Common to all three types of conveyances is the requirement for the purchaser to bear a cost which will benefit the transferor to the extent revenue is produced from his retained interest. The cost of carrying out the commitment to the transferor is directly related to the minerals-in-place to which the purchaser has acquired title, for that commitment is a part of the consideration for transfer of mineral rights. The full measure of the consideration given to acquire properties includes the estimated cost of services to be performed as a commitment under the purchase agreement.

The practice followed by some purchasers in ABC transactions of recording the face amount of the retained production payment as part of the cost of mineral rights obtained, with an equivalent amount credited to liabilities, is not consistent with the conventional definition of cost. The purchaser assumes a commitment to produce the minerals conveyed to a third person by the seller but he never acquires title to the reserved mineral interest. The purchaser must bear the entire cost of production but the portion of revenue accruing to the reserved mineral interest belongs to someone else.

Seller. The transferor of rights in a farm-out makes no accounting entry for development costs incurred by the operator. If production is obtained, the entire cost of the transferor's original interest is recorded in a producing property account and is amortized over production and sale of the minerals pertaining to his remaining interest.

The transferor of rights (the carried interest) in a carried-interest arrangement is in a slightly different position. If production is obtained, revenue from the minerals to which he retains title is foregone until his share of development costs is recovered by the operator (purchaser). In those circumstances the carried interest has given something of value—minerals produced—in exchange for a continuing interest in the facilities used to produce additional minerals to which he has title. The carried interest must determine whether to report expenditures incurred for his account by the developer-operator as value received in exchange for the mineral interest conveyed to the developer-operator or whether to maintain memorandum records only.

In the first alternative, the carried interest must decide at what point to credit income with the costs charged to his interest. Should income be credited as expenditures are made or as they are recovered through production? Or should costs be deferred and credited to income ratably over the life of the mineral reserves?

Under the second alternative, the carried interest must decide whether to transpose memorandum records to financial records if the venture proves successful and recovery of cost is assured and, if so, how to record the corresponding credit.

The answer to these questions of fair reporting by the carried interest for his participation in development expenditures lies in defining what he receives in exchange for the interest conveyed to the developer-operator. By agreement, he receives development of his interest without further cost to him except to the extent that his portion of revenue from production is retained by the developer-operator. If no production is obtained, the carried interest has nothing to record except loss of his investment in the undeveloped leasehold. If the venture is successful, the carried interest receives an interest in the capital facilities through which mineral reserves will be produced and sold. Whatever benefit those expenditures have lies in the underlying minerals.

Two points emerge from these considerations. First, the carried interest receives value in exchange for the interest conveyed to the developer-operator, consisting of facilities through which minerals can be produced. Second, the facilities are associated with all developed reserves of the property, not only the portion from which the developer-operator recovers expenditures made on behalf of the carried interest.

The carried interest should record these facts by capitalizing his portion of expenditures as those expenditures are recovered through production by the developer-operator, with corresponding credits to income. As a condition for capitalization, the facts should demonstrate a reasonable expectation of future revenue sufficient to realize whatever amounts are capitalized. The capitalized costs should be amortized by charges to income ratably over the production and sale of underlying reserves.

It would be inconsistent with this view for the developer-operator to record as revenue the portion of sales from which costs related to the carried interest are recovered. Costs incurred by the developer-operator on behalf of the carried interest should be deferred and reduced periodically by sales proceeds attributable to the carried interest.

Sales of Continuing Fractional Interests

The previous discussion, particularly the summary of accounting practices in Table 5, page 103, indicates the wide variety of possible divisions and sales of mineral interests and related accounting practices.

To recapitulate, conveyances of continuing partial mineral interests for cash (which do not include carved-out production payments, previously discussed) are made from both undeveloped and producing properties, and the rights conveyed may be a working interest, a nonoperating interest, or any part or combination of the two. In some cases, proceeds may be pledged for development of the property.

In practice, three methods of accounting for these conveyances by the grantor have been developed: (1) credit the proceeds to grantor's property costs; (2) allocate a pro rata part of grantor's costs to the interest sold and recognize any profit (but not loss); (3) record all proceeds as income with no charge for any portion of property costs (applied only to undeveloped properties). There is some tendency to favor the first method over the second method when undeveloped property is involved.

The first method reflects the nature of many of these transactions as a means of sharing the risks in mineral ventures—of recovering a portion of costs which otherwise might have to be borne entirely by the grantor. Although the element of risk is common to both undeveloped and producing properties, it is greater for undeveloped properties. The difference in relative degree of risk may account for the somewhat greater popularity of this method of accounting for undeveloped properties.

The first method, however—crediting the proceeds to grantor's property costs—is not inherently sound as is apparent in the ultimate situation when a fractional interest may be sold for more than the grantor's property cost. The method breaks down when all cost is recovered and the remainder of the proceeds must be credited to income. Although extreme, these circumstances result from a shortcoming inherent in the method itself which must therefore exist in all cases, whether or not extreme.

Furthermore, the method is not consistent with the concept of investment in mining properties as a cost of potential or proved underlying mineral reserves. Since the investment pertains to all minerals in the property unit, reduction of ownership interest in potential or proved mineral reserves by sale of a fractional interest in the unit should also reduce the cost of the remaining investment to a proportionate amount of the cost of the original interest.

Consistency and logic support the practice of allocating cost to the interest sold and recognizing the difference between cost and proceeds as income or loss. At present, under the allocation-of-cost alternative, income but not loss usually is recognized at the time of sale. This distinction is difficult to support, except as recognition of the risk-sharing aspect of these transactions. However, when the proceeds are less than the amount of a reasonable allocation of cost, the transaction appears to cast doubt on the value of the entire property and to suggest a reduction in the capitalized cost of the remaining property interest. Unless there is some reason to believe that the proceeds from the sale of a partial interest are not representative of the value of the remainder, a proportional loss should be recorded on the *entire* investment.

Measurement of the appropriate amount of cost to be allocated to a fractional interest can be difficult. Cost should be split in the same proportion as interest sold and interest retained. When a fraction of the working interest is sold, the calculation is uncomplicated because the interest sold and the interest retained are homogeneous. If a nonoperating interest is sold and a working interest is retained, the calculation is complicated by the dissimilarities between the types of interests. A nonoperating interest is not burdened by costs, and presumably is more valuable than the same fraction of ownership in a working interest. The answer to this problem lies in allocation of cost on the basis of estimated values of the interests conveyed and retained.

The third method—crediting proceeds to income with no corresponding charge for a portion of investment cost—is used by a minority and is supported only by expediency in the face of difficult allocation problems. It allows no recognition of what has been given up by the seller in exchange for the amount recorded as income. An estimate of proportionate cost should be made and charged against income if proper matching is to be obtained.

A variation in sales of fractional interests is introduced when proceeds are pledged to development of the property. The restriction added has connotations of a sharing of cost rather than sale of an asset. A majority of petroleum companies treats the transaction as a cost-sharing arrangement by reporting the proceeds as a reduction of development costs. The prescribed accounting for federal income tax purposes is to reduce development costs.

The arrangement, however, does not provide for participation in actual development costs by the purchaser. The amount of proceeds is fixed, and any deficiency or excess over allocable cost of the fractional interest sold remains the responsibility of the grantor-operator. The sharing aspect is limited to application of the proceeds. A commitment to apply proceeds to a particular purpose appears not to alter the nature of the transaction from essentially that of a sale. This study therefore recommends:

> **Recommendation 15.** *Sales of continuing fractional interests in mineral properties for cash should be recorded as revenue and a proportionate share of property costs should be charged against revenue so that the net gain or loss is reflected in income.*

7

Accounting for Federal Income Taxes

The important sources of differences between book and tax income peculiar to extractive operations are the following:

1. Percentage depletion in excess of cost depletion.
2. Geological and geophysical costs directly related to acquisition of property, which must be capitalized for tax purposes.
3. Costs of successful exploration in mining industries other than oil and gas, which may be deducted (with limitations) as incurred for tax purposes.
4. Intangible drilling and development costs on successful wells in the petroleum industry, which may be deducted as incurred for tax purposes.
5. Development expenditures capitalized during the production stage of mineral properties, other than oil and gas, which may be deducted as incurred for tax purposes.
6. Future lifting costs of production to satisfy a retained mineral interest payment when capitalized in an ABC transaction, which must be deducted when incurred for tax purposes.
7. Sale of carved-out production payment, proceeds from which must be recorded in taxable income in the year of sale.
8. Amortization of cost of undeveloped properties, which is not deductible for tax purposes.
9. Deferral of a portion of revenue under take-or-pay con-

tracts, or of gas revenue subject to approval of contract price increase, both of which are includable in taxable income in the year that revenue accrues according to the sales contracts.

The extractive industries are affected in various degrees by these differences between book and tax income. The petroleum industry is affected more than most of the others. In extractive industries other than the petroleum industry, tax and financial accounting practices tend to coincide. For example, most mining companies other than petroleum companies charge the major part of development costs and all receding face costs during the production stage to operations as incurred for financial accounting as well as tax purposes. The corresponding item in the petroleum industry, IDC, is usually capitalized for financial accounting when wells are successful, but is almost always deducted for tax purposes as incurred.

Mining companies other than petroleum occasionally capitalize unusually extensive development expenditures, even during the production stage, when the expenditures prepare ore beds for several years' production. A credit equivalent to the tax effect is usually reflected as a reduction in the deferral of expenditures or separately in a deferred tax account. Similarly, for other differences, these mining companies have practiced interperiod income tax allocation rather generally.

The petroleum industry, in which almost all the possible differences listed above occur most frequently, has been less inclined to practice interperiod income tax allocation. In general, these companies have tended (prior to *APB Opinion 11*) to confine tax allocation to those items which are expressly covered by existing AICPA pronouncements, that is, large nonrecurring items and accelerated and guideline depreciation differences of material amount. The results of the API survey on this subject are shown in Table 1, opposite.

To determine the changes in present practice required to conform to *APB Opinion 11*, the tax effect of each item listed on page 113 must be identified either as a permanent difference or a timing difference. Each item is discussed below in that context.

Percentage Depletion

Although the excess of percentage over cost depletion was acknowledged in *APB Opinion 11* to be a permanent difference for which no

CHAPTER 7: ACCOUNTING FOR FEDERAL INCOME TAXES

SUMMARY OF INCOME TAX ALLOCATIONS

TABLE 1

Type of Transaction	Not Applicable	Book and Tax Treatment Same	Book and Tax Treatment Different	Allocate Tax Yes	Allocate Tax No
(Number of Companies*)					
Intangible Drilling Costs on Successful Wells	1	2	26	1	25
Significant Items on Which Tax Allocation Is Practiced by 10 Companies or More:					
Accelerated depreciation	5	3	21	16	5
Reserves for possible refund of gas revenue pending rate determination	8	—	21	10	11
Carved-out oil payments	7	—	22	17	5
Items on Which Tax Allocation Is Practiced by 4 Companies or Less:					
Amortization of the cost of unoperated acreage	15	—	14	4	10
Reserves for various employee benefits	19	—	10	4	6
Reserves for self-insurance	18	—	11	2	9
Refinery turnarounds, tanker surveys, etc.	12	—	17	2	15
Purchase of a property subject to a reserved production payment when the cash outlay plus lifting costs have been capitalized	17	—	12	2	10
Outside geological and geophysical costs capitalized for tax purposes and expensed for book purposes	—	13	16	1	15
Items on Which Tax Allocation Is Not Practiced:					
Gas injection costs	2	26	1	—	1
Leasing costs	—	24	5	—	5
Carrying costs, items capitalized for tax purposes and expensed for book purposes	—	24	5	—	5
Reserves for bad debts	—	19	10	—	10
Partial surrenders of leases	3	20	6	—	6
Amortization of goodwill and other intangible assets	15	—	14	—	14
Preoperational expenses	4	24	1	—	1
Inventory costing procedures	—	26	3	—	3
Purchase of a property subject to a reserved production payment when the cash outlay plus the face value of the production payment has been capitalized	27	—	2	—	2
Research and development costs	2	27	—	—	—

*Data based on replies from 29 companies.

Source: American Petroleum Institute, *Report of Certain Petroleum Industry Accounting Practices*, 1965, p. 75.

tax allocation is required, its function should be discussed here to appreciate its corollary effects on some of the other tax differences.

For tax purposes, percentage depletion is an alternative to depletion based on property cost. Property cost includes acquisition costs such as lease bonuses or fee purchase and that portion of geological and geophysical costs which relates directly to acquisition of property. Cost depletion seldom exceeds percentage depletion except perhaps when a mineral property already in production is purchased.

Percentage depletion is applied to gross income from all mineral production, except those minerals which are in limitless, accessible supply, for example, sod and dirt. The rates of depletion range from 5% for sand and gravel to 27½% for petroleum and natural gas. The particular percentage for any one mineral is intended to represent the estimated measure of risk attendant to discovery. Percentage depletion is limited to 50% of net (taxable) income from the mining property computed without the depletion charge.

Because of the 50% limitation on percentage depletion, companies seldom obtain full benefit of the statutory percentage depletion rates. Petroleum companies, for example, usually experience an overall depletion rate amounting to about 22% to 23% of gross income, whereas the statutory percentage depletion rate is 27½%.

The depletion allowable for tax purposes may, therefore, be on any of three bases: cost, percentage of revenue, or percentage of revenue limited to 50% of taxable net income. Since the determination is made separately for each property unit, as defined in the Internal Revenue Code, it is probable that total allowable depletion in any one year, when the taxpayer owns several property units, will consist of an aggregate of amounts calculated on each of the three bases. These alternative bases of calculating depletion are illustrated by the example in Table 2, opposite, of allowable depletion on an oil lease in which varying factors are assumed (for illustrative purposes only). The allowable depletion in each alternative is underscored. The tax basis must be reduced by allowable depletion; reduction to a zero tax basis eliminates cost depletion but does not limit future percentage depletion.

Geological and Geophysical Costs

Geological and geophysical costs directly related to the acquisition of property rights must be capitalized for tax purposes as part of property cost subject to depletion even though they are more com-

TABLE 2

Alternative Bases for Calculating Allowable Depletion on an Oil Lease

Assumptions	A	Alternative B	C
Reserves at beginning of year (bbls.)	3,000,000	3,000,000	3,000,000
Production (bbls.)	400,000	300,000	250,000
Remaining undepleted cost (tax basis) at beginning of year	$1,000,000	$1,000,000	$3,000,000
Gross income	$1,500,000	$1,150,000	$ 950,000
Operating expenses	$ 500,000	$ 600,000	$ 500,000
Net income before depletion	$1,000,000	$ 550,000	$ 450,000
Allowable depletion:			
27½% of gross income	$ 412,500	$ 316,250	$ 261,250
50% of "net" income	$ 500,000	$ 275,000	$ 225,000
Cost	$ 133,333	$ 100,000	$ 250,000

monly charged to expense as incurred in financial statements. In practice, the Internal Revenue Service tends to require only outside contracted costs to be so deferred.

The major portion of geological and geophysical costs capitalized proves to be associated with unsuccessful projects. Such costs are deductible for tax purposes when the property is abandoned. Capitalized geological and geophysical costs which prove to be associated with a producing property (the lesser portion) are subject to depletion over the life of the mineral reserves. Unless cost depletion exceeds percentage depletion, no reduction in income taxes will result from these depletion charges.

Assuming that all geological and geophysical costs are charged to expense as incurred, the portion initially capitalized for income tax purposes that is subsequently identified with abandoned properties creates a tax timing difference, and the remaining portion initially capitalized for income tax purposes that is subsequently identified with producing properties creates a permanent tax difference. *APB Opinion 11* requires recording of prepaid income tax in the year these costs were charged to financial statement expense but capitalized for tax purposes, but the amount of the prepaid tax is limited to the tax effect of that portion of geological and geophysical costs which will finally be identified with abandoned properties. Prepaid tax should not be recorded for the effect of that portion of geological and geophysical costs which will finally be identified with producing properties except to the extent that cost depletion will exceed percentage depletion for tax purposes. That possibility is remote in most cases.

Costs of Successful Exploration— Other Than Oil and Gas

Costs of successful exploration in extractive industries other than oil and gas may be deducted as incurred up to $100,000 in any one year, limited to a total of $400,000 over the life of the taxpayer. As an alternative, the taxpayer may elect to write off all exploration costs when incurred without regard to the $100,000 and $400,000 limitation but the resulting deductions are then subject to recapture by including the amounts in gross income or by foregoing depletion in equal amount after the mine enters the producing stage.

If the option to defer exploration costs is taken, the amounts are required to be amortized ratably over total reserves as they are produced but they are excluded from the property base upon which depletion is calculated. Thus, whether deducted as incurred or deferred, these costs are subject to recovery as ordinary deductions, not through depletion. Under either option discussed in the preceding paragraph, a tax timing difference is created and tax allocation is required except to the extent that deduction of exploration costs as incurred will increase future percentage depletion by reducing future amortization charges that otherwise would have limited percentage depletion under the 50% of net income limitation. To that extent, a permanent tax difference is created.

IDC on Successful Wells in the Petroleum Industry

Oil and gas taxpayers are entitled to deduct the intangible drilling and development costs associated with successful exploratory and development wells as the costs are incurred. If this option is not taken, most of the IDC then becomes a part of property cost subject to depletion, and hence part of the cost depletion alternative to percentage depletion. If elected as a deduction in the year incurred, the charge enters into the determination of net income for purposes of computing the 50% limitation on percentage depletion from each property unit; however, it is not considered an element of cost depletion in that year. Thus, immediate deduction of IDC can reduce percentage depletion in the year of incurrence. The practical effect is usually not great since most of these costs are incurred during the initial development stage of a property when net income is small or nonexistent.

The example in Table 2 on page 117 is used to illustrate the effect of an expenditure for intangible drilling and development costs. The election to deduct IDC as incurred would increase ordinary deductions from taxable income arising from all sources in that year but would also reduce allowable percentage depletion to whatever extent it might trigger the 50% of net income limitation on percentage depletion from the property upon which the IDC was incurred. Thus, in the illustration, if IDC expenditures of $200,000 were deducted, allowable depletion would be reduced under Alternative A from $412,500 to $400,000 (50% of $800,000—net income before depletion of $1,000,000 reduced by the $200,000 additional cost), and under Alternative B from $275,000 to $175,000. Alternative C would not be affected since allowable depletion is based on capitalized cost.

If, on the other hand, IDC were not deducted as incurred but were capitalized and depleted, the taxpayer would forego the ordinary deduction from taxable income in the year of expenditure and would recover the cost in subsequent years only if cost depletion were higher than percentage depletion. In the example above, assuming that an IDC expenditure of $200,000 had been capitalized for tax purposes as of the beginning of the year, only Alternative C would be affected by cost depletion on IDC capitalized. In that case, allowable depletion would be increased from $250,000 to $266,667. (For illustration, all capitalized IDC is assumed depletable.) The net tax effect of alternative IDC elections in the year of expenditure is summarized in Table 3, page 120.

If IDC were capitalized, theoretically there might be tax benefit in future years to whatever extent IDC would cause cost depletion on the property involved to exceed percentage depletion. In practice, cost depletion rarely exceeds percentage depletion once the property is in full operation. Also, unlike percentage depletion, cost depletion is limited to the amount of the tax basis. Accordingly, as a practical

TABLE 3

Tax Effect of Alternative IDC Elections

	A	Alternative B	C
Immediate deduction:			
48% of additional ordinary deduction of $200,000*	$96,000	$96,000	$96,000
Less—48% of reduction in net income coming under the 50% limitation	6,000	48,000	—
Net benefit	90,000	48,000	96,000
Capitalization:			
48% of effect on cost depletion allowance	—	—	8,000
Net advantage of immediate deduction of IDC	$90,000	$48,000	$88,000

* Assuming sufficient overall corporate taxable net income from other properties or sources.

matter, IDC expenditures should almost always be deducted in the year of incurrence to obtain the ultimate maximum tax benefit. By that means, the taxpayer will obtain a deduction from ordinary taxable income without a commensurate increase in future taxable income since future calculations of percentage depletion will not be affected. The deduction would be lost if the election were made to capitalize and deplete the expenditure.

Successful intangible drilling and development costs are distinguishable from differences of a timing nature because the allowable deduction is effectively lost unless the option to charge the expenditure off as incurred is elected. When the tax laws permit a similar election with regard to other deductions, such as accelerated depreciation, the election determines the periods which will receive the tax benefit of the deduction but does not, of itself, change the amount. In contrast, the tax effect from deduction of intangible drilling and development costs is not available as a practical matter unless the deduction is taken in the period in which the costs are incurred. The tax effect of immediate deduction is not borrowed from the future—it would never have existed had the deduction not been made.

It should be noted, however, that some portion of IDC relates to depreciable equipment, rather than depletable property costs and, if capitalized, would be recoverable through depreciation. Expenditures for wages, fuel, repairs, hauling, supplies, etc., used in installation of casing and equipment in oil or gas wells, are examples of depreciable costs, whereas expenditures for clearing ground, draining, road making, surveying, geological work, drilling, shooting, and cleaning of wells are depletable costs. The amount of IDC assignable to depreciable costs is usually relatively small.

Unless some unusual circumstances exist, the tax reduction from an immediate deduction of intangible drilling and development costs is, in fact, permanent and therefore provides no basis for interperiod allocation of income taxes under *APB Opinion 11.*

Some advocates of interperiod tax allocation, however, believe it is not always necessary to demonstrate that a tax difference is temporary in order to justify deferral. They reason that tax effects which can be identified with specific assets should be attached to the cost of those assets. If the asset is amortized over future periods, so should the related tax effect even though of itself it might be a permanent tax difference. This concept appears in *APB Opinion 2,* "Accounting for the 'Investment Credit,'" where advocates of deferring the tax effect of the investment tax credit state: ". . . earnings arise from the use of facilities, not from their acquisition."

Both the investment tax credit (ITC) and IDC, as demonstrated above, create permanent tax differences. In either case, the tax reduction is obtainable only when the expenditures are made (subject, of course, to net operating loss carrybacks or carryforwards). The reductions in tax are fully realized at that time and no contingency on their use remains. Since the tax transaction itself is completed, deferral can be justified only if it is required to obtain better matching of effort (cost) and result (revenue). As described in Chapter 3, the matching process requires that cost be attached to specific revenue when there is an observable relationship between effort and result.

The tax effects of IDC and ITC cannot be identified directly with future revenue. If a direct revenue relationship were to be sought for these tax reductions, it would be more logical to identify them with current revenue which is the starting point in calculating income tax.

In the absence of a direct relationship to future revenue, deferral of the tax effects of IDC would be required only if they were elements of the cost of productive capacity which are capitalized because the facility will produce revenue in future periods. This is a question of definition of cost—a question implied, although not stated, in the quotation above from *APB Opinion 2* supporting deferral of the investment tax credit.

The deduction of IDC for tax purposes does not create a cost element. IDC as a tax deduction is only one of many components affecting the amount of tax payable. IDC enters into the tax transaction as a matter of tax policy rather than as part of the cost of the transaction between the taxpayer and the taxing entity. In this, IDC is not distinguishable from other items affecting taxable income. The components of taxable income are governed by tax laws and regulations which are influenced by the total need for tax revenue, by the desired allocation of tax burden among classes of taxpayers and by considerations of economic policy. Tax laws are not concerned with the matching of revenue and expense as an objective except as it may be consistent with the aforementioned influences. Whatever the outcome, the resulting tax payable is a cost of doing business in that taxable year. There is no identifiable cause-and-effect relationship with revenue of any other period.

The IDC transaction in its own right is for a specific purpose—to create productive facilities for creation of future revenue. An exchange of assets takes place, properly measurable under the cost convention by cash expenditures or the cash equivalent of obligations and commitments made to suppliers of the facilities. There is no apparent convention or logic to support reducing the costs of those transactions with those suppliers by the amount of a transaction with an unrelated person (the taxing entity) for an unrelated purpose.

Development Expenditures During the Production Stage of Mines

After a mine (other than oil and gas properties) enters the production stage, all development costs can be deducted currently as ordinary operating expenses (development costs include "receding face costs"—equipment costs of a capital nature which are incurred to maintain rather than increase production). On the other hand, the taxpayer may elect to defer development costs and to amortize them over the life of the mine. In either case, charges are deductible in addition to, not as an alternative to, percentage depletion. The distinction between these development costs and capitalized IDC on oil and gas properties should be noted. Although both mine development costs and IDC may be capitalized at the taxpayer's option, the probabilities of reducing future taxable income by the amortization charges are quite different. Deductions for IDC are an either/or proposition with percentage depletion, and the latter almost always is greater. Deductions from taxable income for the amortization of capitalized development costs may be made in addition to percentage depletion.

On the other hand, development costs are deductible from gross income for purposes of determining the 50% of net income limitation on percentage depletion. An increase in percentage depletion in future years as a result of electing to deduct development costs currently for tax purposes is therefore possible. That situation occurs to whatever extent the amortization charges in future years would have limited percentage depletion had the alternative election of amortization been made.

Accordingly, the tax difference created by deferring development costs in the financial statements but electing to deduct them immediately for tax purposes may be partly temporary and partly permanent. The temporary portion, but not any permanent portion, of the tax reduction should be deferred to the future periods over which deferred costs are amortized.

Future Lifting Costs of Production to Satisfy a Retained Mineral Interest Payment

The buyer of a property subject to a reserved production payment can capitalize only the cash portion of the purchase price for tax purposes. During the period of satisfying the reserved payment from production, the buyer includes in taxable income only his share of income (excluding the seller's reserved production payment share). All production costs, including those applicable to the reserved payment interest, are borne by the buyer and are deductible for tax purposes as incurred.[1]

When estimated production costs applicable to the reserved payment are capitalized for financial statement purposes (the recommended treatment), the estimated lifting costs involved are amortized in the financial statements over the entire life of the reserves to which the buyer has title. Since they are deductible for tax purposes during the shorter period of years required to satisfy the reserved minerals payment, a tax timing difference is created. These costs share the

---

[1] A long-standing practice which has been brought into question recently in two Tax Court cases: *L. W. Brooke, Jr.*, paragraph 50.94, P.H.T.C., and *Producers Chemical Company*, paragraph 50.95, P.H.T.C. The Tax Court concluded that operating expenses allocable to the retained interest should be capitalized as part of the cost of acquiring the working interest.

same tax distinction from IDC as development expenditures during the production stage of mines, discussed previously.

Sale of a Carved-Out Production Payment

Reporting proceeds from sale of a carved-out production payment as revenue in later periods when the underlying minerals are produced, as recommended, gives rise to a tax timing difference, since the proceeds are includable in taxable income during the year of sale. When the 50% of net income limitation on percentage depletion is in effect, however, part of the tax effect may become a permanent difference to which allocation requirements of *APB Opinion 11* should not apply.

Maximizing the 50% of net income limitation on percentage depletion is possible by the sale of a carved-out production payment from a property if that limitation would otherwise apply. The feasibility of such a transaction, of course, depends on whether a buyer can be found and whether other economic and operating factors associated with satisfying the production payment are favorable.

The example in Table 2, page 117, is used to illustrate the possible effect of the sale of a carved-out production payment on percentage depletion allowed. In the example, under Alternative B, allowable depletion was held to $275,000, as limited by 50% of net income. The limit could be raised by increasing income from the property through the use of a production payment; the maximum effect is reached when the income is increased sufficiently to bring the 50% of net income limitation up to the 27½% depletion rate. A production payment sale of $183,000 [2] would approximate the optimum results. The effect on allowable depletion of the sale of a carved-out production payment in that amount is illustrated in Table 4, opposite.

The full percentage depletion rate of 27½% on the production payment proceeds alone would have produced only $50,325 more allowable depletion. The difference between this and the actual increase of $91,500 in allowable depletion after the sale of the produc-

---

[2] The formula by which this amount can be determined is the amount of the difference between depletion at 27½% and depletion limited to 50% of net income divided by 22½% (50% − 27½%). Thus, in the illustration, depletion lost by 50% of net income limitation was $41,250 (see Table 2, page 117) which, when divided by 22½%, produces $183,333.

TABLE 4

Effect on Allowable Depletion of the Sale of a Carved-Out Production Payment

	Before Sale of Production Payment	After Sale of Production Payment
Gross income	$1,150,000	$1,333,000
Operating expenses	600,000	600,000
Net income before depletion	550,000	733,000
Allowable depletion (underscored)		
27½% of gross income	$ 316,250	$ 366,575
50% of "net" income	275,000	366,500

tion payment is attributable to maximizing the 50% of net income limitation, thereby "saving" percentage depletion which otherwise would have been lost. In the foregoing illustration, the overall reduction in income tax is $19,764 ($91,500 − $50,325 = $41,175; $41,175 × .48 = $19,764).

Of course, if the "borrowing" of revenue by means of the production payment sale reduces taxable income in future years sufficiently to cause the 50% of net income limitation to become effective in those years, some of the percentage depletion "saved" in the year of production payment sale might prove to be offset by a corresponding reduction in allowable percentage depletion in future years. As long as the remaining future revenue from the property is sufficient to maintain allowable depletion at the full 27½% rate, no corresponding reduction will occur.

Since the proceeds from sale of a production payment should be reported in revenue as the underlying minerals are produced, a tax difference arises. In the circumstances described above, the difference is in part permanent and in part temporary. Although the proceeds from sale of the production payment are subject to tax at the full statutory rate, and this by itself is a timing difference, the interplay with percentage depletion in the circumstances described creates an additional permanent tax reduction that lowers the overall tax expense. The actual tax increase in the year of sale is therefore significantly less than the gross amount of tax attributable to the proceeds from the sale of the carved-out production payment.

The overall tax increase in the year of sale ($43,920) is computed as follows:

Production payment proceeds		$183,000
Less—Increase in depletion because of production payment:		
Depletion after	$366,500	
Depletion before	275,000	
		91,500
Net increase in taxable income		$ 91,500
Tax at 48%		$ 43,920

The net tax increase method of allocation, based on the $43,920, is now most commonly used to calculate the amount of tax to be deferred to future periods. It conforms to the methodology of *APB Opinion 11* (paragraph 36), since it is the "differential between income taxes computed with and without inclusion of the transaction creating the difference between taxable income and pretax accounting income."

This method results, however, in transferring the full reduction in income tax attributable to the additional percentage depletion to future periods thereby ignoring completely the permanent character of percentage depletion tax effects in the year of sale. Since *APB Opinion 11* recognizes the tax reduction from percentage depletion as a permanent difference not requiring allocation, there should be some recognition that income reported for the year of sale has been increased by a permanent reduction in tax.

That result could be obtained by allocating tax to future periods at the full statutory rate applied to total proceeds, as follows:

Production payment proceeds	$183,000
Less—Percentage depletion at 27½%, a permanent difference	50,325
Increase in taxable income	132,675
Tax at 48%, to be deferred as a prepaid item	$ 63,684

This method corresponds to the concept of reporting permanent tax differences as a reduction of tax expense in the year they are obtained; it credits tax expense for the year of sale with the gross amount of tax attributable to the production payment proceeds, including the amount of tax reduction from additional percentage depletion that would have been lost had the sale not been made. The tax allocated to future years will exceed the tax effect of the sale by the amount of tax on percentage depletion saved in the year of sale.

The second method, based on tax effect of $63,684, is recommended because it conforms to the concept in *APB Opinion 11*. Each of the two methods described, however, conflicts in part with *APB Opinion 11*. The first method complies with methodology but conflicts with concept; the second method complies with concept but conflicts with methodology. The interplay of gross income from the production payment and other gross income creates an additional permanent tax difference as well as a timing difference.

In the illustration given, percentage depletion in future years presumably will not be reduced by advancing revenue to the current period through the sale of the production payment. To the extent that this result cannot be reasonably predicted, the amount of tax allocated to future years should be correspondingly reduced.

Amortization of Cost of Undeveloped Properties

Amortization charges for estimated losses on capitalized costs of undeveloped properties are not deductible for federal income tax purposes. Abandonment is required to establish a deduction. The tax difference created by the nondeductible amortization charges is a timing difference subject to interperiod allocation.

However, if the estimate of loss proves to be unfounded and properties become productive, recording of a future tax effect from current amortization charges would have created accumulated debit balances that would never be realized through tax reductions if percentage depletion is effective. Capitalized costs of properties which prove to be productive are deductible through depletion, and cost depletion seldom exceeds percentage depletion. The basic reporting error in these circumstances is the anticipation of a loss in undeveloped property investments which did not occur. In retrospect, the charges for amortization of cost of undeveloped properties should not have been made. The fact that the effect of these amortization charges was reduced by anticipation of a tax effect mitigates the error. Therefore, the possibility that investments in unproven properties might give rise to percentage depletion deductions rather than anticipated abandonment loss deductions should not influence the reporting of prepaid tax related to amortization charges prior to proving the existence of mineral reserves.

Revenue from Take-or-Pay Contracts and Gas Contract Price Increases Subject to Approval

Revenue under take-or-pay contracts and gas sales at price increases not yet approved by the Federal Power Commission is includable in taxable income in the year received despite the potential commitment to deliver additional minerals without further charge or to refund disallowed prices. To the extent that the revenue is deferred for financial reports, a difference from taxable income is created. The difference causes an accumulation of taxes paid during the periods revenue is deferred in financial reports with corresponding relief of tax expense during subsequent periods. Accordingly, the tax differences are essentially of a timing nature and should be allocated among appropriate periods. If, however, the revenue tends to increase the percentage depletion allowance when the 50% net income limitation is otherwise in effect, a corresponding part of the tax effect should be considered permanent (see the discussion on carved-out production payments on pages 124 to 127).

Summary and Conclusions

In the preceding discussion, tax differences have been analyzed in terms of the standards prescribed by *APB Opinion 11*. Two of the differences are wholly permanent. For these items, no allocation of tax effect is required:

1. Percentage depletion.

2. Intangible drilling and development costs.

Two of the differences are wholly temporary. For these items, interperiod allocation of tax effect is required:

1. Lifting costs capitalized in connection with ABC transactions.

2. Amortization of undeveloped property costs.

Five items contain a mixture of permanent and temporary tax differences; allocation of only the timing difference portion is recommended:

1. Geological and geophysical costs directly related to acquisition of property.
2. Successful exploration and development costs of mineral properties other than oil and gas.
3. Revenue from sale of carved-out production payments to maximize allowable percentage depletion.
4. Revenue from take-or-pay contracts.
5. Revenue from gas contract price increases subject to approval.

* * * * * * * * * * * * *

FOOTNOTE TO CHAPTER 7

The complications involved in applying *APB Opinion 11* to extractive operations must add to the doubts which many share as to the soundness of the concept of comprehensive tax allocation adopted by the Accounting Principles Board.

In considering the desirability of interperiod allocation of income taxes, one fact ought to be recognized: within the limits of estimate, the actual amount of income tax payable for any one period is a known quantity determinable by application of tax laws then in effect. The amount of the transaction between taxpayer and federal government is established at that point and there is no legal basis for representing in the financial statements that income tax expense, as such, is either a greater or a lesser amount.

Recording tax liabilities which do not exist can be justified for substantial differences between accounting and tax income which will definitely reverse in the relatively near future. In that case, a reasonably determinable increase or decrease in future tax expense can be foreseen from current transactions. In those circumstances, to report the transaction in one period and the tax effect in another could be misleading.

On the other hand, if continuing transactions form a recurring pattern of timing differences between financial statement and tax income, a permanent deferral or accrual of income tax is effectively created. In those circumstances, tax effect accounting would result in an accumulation of deferred credits or debits which would finally stabilize in amount at the end of the first cycle of amortization. At that point the amortization of previously deferred amounts to operations approximates the charge or credit for deferral of tax effect of current transactions, and reported income approximates the amount it would have been had allocation not been adopted. The result is a permanent reduction or increase in retained earnings. The corresponding deferred charges and credits in the balance sheet relate to future events so remote as to represent nothing more than contingencies. Consequently, the Opinion is not consistent with the concept of financial reporting as a representation of fact and it departs from both the cost and realization conventions which require an exchange to take place before expenditures and revenue are recorded.

8

Presentation of Financial Statements and Disclosure of Supplementary Information in Financial Reports

The recommendations of this chapter are based on a review of the 1964 annual reports of 265 companies (listed in Appendix C) supplemented by a review of the Form 10-K reports to the Securities and Exchange Commission for 69 of the companies.[1] The following tabulation classifies the companies by primary activity and shows the number of companies in each class whose annual reports and Form 10-K reports were reviewed.

	Number of Companies	
Primary Activity	Annual Report	Form 10-K
Integrated petroleum	54	28*
Nonintegrated petroleum	56	
Iron	25	8
Nonferrous metal	61	14
Coal	18	5
Bauxite, asbestos, and uranium	10	4
Salt, sulfur, and potash	8	2
Cement, stone, gravel, and sand	33	8
	265	69

* Includes both integrated and nonintegrated petroleum companies.

---

[1] Although disclosure practices from the annual reports of these companies for subsequent years were not summarized, a sufficient number of annual reports of extractive industries companies were reviewed in the course of the research and writing of this study to indicate that the practices found are reasonably representative of current practice.

In those cases in which both the annual report and the Form 10-K of a company were reviewed, the reports were compared to determine whether disclosure in them differed materially. Also, if prospectuses of these companies were available, they were compared to the annual report and the Form 10-K.

The reports contain a variety of practices regarding details in financial statements, description of accounting practices, and disclosure of other operating data including information on mineral properties and reserves. The review indicates that standards of appropriate disclosure should be established.

The complex nature and uncertainties of extractive operations are manifested in a variety of accounting practices for what appear to be similar transactions. These alternatives indicate the need for a description in financial statements of accounting practices with regard to each significant type of transaction, at least until such time as agreement on a single accounting practice is reached. Even then, because of the complexity of operations, the usefulness of the financial statements will be enhanced by disclosure of unusual or particularly significant transactions and the manner in which they have been reported.

The process of finding minerals presents very difficult problems in reporting to investors. The process requires substantial expenditures for the discovery of economically recoverable reserves, with a wide range of possible results; similarly, subsequent development to fully define reserves may require additional heavy expenditures. Under these circumstances, presenting financial statements without disclosing some supplementary information relating to recoverable reserves may not represent adequate reporting to investors. Moreover, supplementing reserve data by describing related physical activities and classifying related expenditures in the financial statements to show the magnitude of effort would further enhance the usefulness of financial reports to investors.

This chapter recommends disclosure practices to deal with the especially difficult or unique reporting problems of extractive industries without intending that the recommendations should apply with equal force to all extractive companies. What constitutes significant disclosure in some company operations may not be significant in others, as illustrated by the discussion of varying significance of mineral reserves in Chapter 3. Furthermore, the recommendations are not intended to disclose information that would give competitors an advantage not otherwise obtainable. This result would not be in the best interest of stockholders.

The following recommendations, therefore, should be read as generalized conclusions on what appears to be the most appropriate type of disclosure in those areas of extractive operations which, in general, have a significance to the investor that is not reflected completely in the financial statements. The recommendations are intended to be guiding rather than governing in all extractive company financial reports.

Description of Major Accounting Policies and Practices

Recommended Practice. The complexity of operations of the extractive industries leads to the following recommendation:

> **Recommendation 16.** *A description of major accounting policies and practices should be included in notes to financial statements.*

Financial statements should be supplemented by description of company accounting policy for each major element of revenue or expenditure which contains implications of benefit to more than one period with respect to the following key accounting decisions: (1) when revenue is recorded, (2) whether to carry costs forward against future operations, (3) selection of the cost center, and (4) selection of method and basis for allocation of items deferred to future periods. Other accounting policies of continuing importance should be included in the statement of general policy.

Additional notes should describe accounting practices for significant specific transactions which occur irregularly, practices which differ from a single preference that is generally accepted, and practices in areas in which substantial authoritative support for two or more alternatives may still exist. This information will facilitate comparison of reports of different companies.

This recommendation for description of accounting policies and practices does not contemplate disclosure of what the financial position or results of operations would have been had some alternative method been used. Presumably, management will have adopted that policy or practice which in its judgment best reflects the circumstances. In that case it would be pointless and confusing to indicate the result of a less appropriate practice.

A general statement of accounting policies and practices might cover the following items:

1. Consolidation practices, including manner of reporting operations of jointly owned affiliated companies.
2. Accounting for prospecting and preliminary exploration costs.
3. Definition of the cost center used for accumulating capitalized property costs.
4. Accounting for capitalized unproven and undeveloped property costs.
5. The policy regarding deferral of costs of successful exploration and development efforts on proven and on producing property units, including the basis for subsequent amortization, and the accounting policy regarding unsuccessful exploration and development costs.
6. The stage in the extractive process at which inventories of minerals are first measured and accounted for in the financial statements.

Present Practices Regarding Description of Major Accounting Policies and Practices. A minority of the companies in the petroleum industry but none of the companies in the other extractive industries gave sufficient description of accounting policy and practice. The frequency of disclosure of accounting policies and practices is summarized in Table 1, opposite.

The almost complete lack of definition of terms is a serious obstacle to evaluation of the financial statements under review. Although some balance sheet and income statement captions are self-explanatory, several important ones are expressed in functional terms which by themselves do not convey a common meaning; for example, expense captions such as "exploration costs" or "development costs." Only a few industries have common accounting manuals by which consistency of classification of exploration or development costs might justifiably be assumed. Without the assurance of a common standard of definition, the reader cannot be sure whether the amounts reported by various companies under functional classifications such as "exploration" or "development" are determined by comparable procedures.

CHAPTER 8: PRESENTATION OF FINANCIAL STATEMENTS AND DISCLOSURE OF SUPPLEMENTARY INFORMATION IN FINANCIAL REPORTS

TABLE 1

Frequency of Disclosure of Accounting Policies and Practices in Annual Reports to Stockholders

	Integrated Petroleum	Nonintegrated Petroleum	Iron	Nonferrous Metal	Coal	Bauxite, Asbestos, and Uranium	Salt, Sulfur, and Potash	Cement, Stone, Gravel, and Sand
Total number of reports reviewed	54	56	25	61	18	10	8	33
General synopsis of accounting policies and practices	9	18	0	0	0	0	0	0
Exploration costs:								
Definition	0	0	0	1	0	0	0	0
Statement of accounting policy	10(1)	19(1)	0	8	0	0	1	0
Acquisition costs:								
Definition	0	0	0	0	0	0	0	0
Statement of accounting policy	7(1)	11(1)	0	0	0	0	0	0
Development costs:								
Definition	1	0	0	0	0	0	0	0
Statement of accounting policy	13(1)	20(1)	0	16	2	3	1	0
Inventory valuation:								
Total showing inventories	53	24	21	54	17	8	8	32
Basis disclosed (cost or market, etc.)	53	23	21	51	17	8	8	32
Basis defined:								
Cost	38 of 53	4 of 12	18 of 21	16 of 33	7 of 16	4 of 8	6 of 8	20 of 32
Market	5 of 50	4 of 18	2 of 21	22 of 46	1 of 15	0 of 7	0 of 6	1 of 28
Depletion and amortization:								
Cost center defined	7(1)	15(1)	0	8	0	1	0	0
Statement of method	14	25	1	10	1	1	0	1
Depreciation:								
Cost center defined	7(1)	13(1)	0	8	0	1	0	0
Statement of method	6	13	3	9	5	3	0	3

(1) Includes, respectively, 6 integrated and 7 nonintegrated petroleum producers which have adopted the "full cost" method.

The tabulation in Table 2, opposite, summarizes the information regarding mineral inventories given in the 265 annual reports to stockholders. Perhaps the most striking feature of inventory reporting is the absence of any statement on inventory policy regarding mined ores. Inventories can be measured and recorded at numerous stages in mining operations. Some petroleum producers measure field stocks, some do not. Other mining industries conceivably could report ore inventories, first measured either in the mine, at the surface, at the crusher, at the concentration plant, or even at the refining plant if that happens to be at the mine site. (Presumably, all ore is inventoried or otherwise accounted for once it is shipped from the mine site.) Inventory positions cannot be compared unless the stage at which inventory is recorded is disclosed.

A general conclusion to be drawn from information in Tables 1 and 2 is that description of accounting policies and methods in annual reports to stockholders is not a common practice. In fact, except for the petroleum industry, almost no disclosure is made of the accounting policies and practices by which the major elements of mining costs are recorded in the financial statements. Some charity is involved in listing 27 petroleum producers as presenting a general synopsis of accounting policies and practices; the basis for the capital/expense decision regarding exploration and development costs is given but other policies such as cost centers and depletion base are usually not described.

Disclosure of Mineral Reserves and Operating Activities

Recommended Practice. Financial statements should be supplemented by information on mineral reserves and operating activities in order to compensate for the limited ability of conventional financial statements to portray the financial position and results of operations of companies in extractive operations. Accordingly, this study recommends:

> **Recommendation 17.** *Mineral reserves and operating activities should be sufficiently disclosed to facilitate evaluation of effort and result.*

As previously discussed in Chapter 3, mineral reserves are important to extractive operations even though the primary significance of reserves might be as a supply of raw materials for further processing

TABLE 2

Frequency of Disclosure of Inventories of Mined Products in Annual Reports to Stockholders

	Integrated Petroleum	Non-integrated Petroleum	Iron	Non-ferrous Metal	Coal	Bauxite, Asbestos, and Uranium	Salt, Sulfur, and Potash	Cement, Stone, Gravel, and Sand	Totals
Extracted minerals shown:									
Separately	4	16	13	37	8	6	5	21	110
Combined with finished products	39	—	5	—	8	—	1	—	53
None shown	—	32	4	7	1	2	—	1	47
Indefinite caption	11	8	3	17	1	2	2	11	55
Totals	54	56	25	61	18	10	8	33	265

rather than as a marketable commodity in its extracted form. The use value or market value of mineral reserves in excess of capitalized discovery and development costs is an "off balance sheet" asset of the enterprise and is a resource of importance to the investor. Reported operating results can be affected substantially by management decisions regarding levels of discovery and development expenditures in relation to reserves discovered and consumed. The effects may not be apparent without disclosure of movements in mineral reserves or disclosure of other operating data.

Also, the lack of relationship between discovery expenditures and resulting mineral quantities and potential market values limits the informational quality of the financial statements in which reserves are not disclosed even though expenditures are stated and appropriately classified between property accounts and expense accounts on the statements.

In general, an extractive company with increasing mineral reserves is probably a better long-term investment prospect than an extractive company with decreasing mineral reserves. Present financial statements do not provide information on this important point. However, to recognize the importance of mineral reserves is one matter—to define their magnitude in terms useful to the investor is another.

The usefulness to the investor of even the most careful estimate of mineral reserves is limited by incomplete knowledge of mineral formations, the uncertainties of measurement techniques, and the economic factors affecting profitability of recovery operations. Typically, many years of further exploration and development are required to gain the knowledge of underground formations, mining conditions, and extent of mineral deposits required for accurate estimates of physically recoverable reserve quantities. In addition, economic factors are important elements in evaluating reserves because minerals which cannot be recovered profitably are worthless. The margin of potential profitability in commercially recoverable mineral reserves can vary substantially depending upon the quality of the mineral, its concentration, its location in relation to markets, and varying underground conditions affecting development and production costs. The effects of the foregoing factors on the quantity of reserves estimated and on the quality of the reserve estimate are compounded by the possibility of technological changes in recovery methods and by changes in markets, including new uses and competitive products which can alter original estimates of commercially recoverable reserves during the typically long periods of exploitation.

Various responses to the problem of how to show mineral reserve resources have been developed or advocated. Responses range from complete silence to recording estimated values of recoverable reserves in the balance sheet.

Silence does not seem to be the answer. A complete absence of information on mineral reserves is illogical in view of the significance of this resource to an extractive company and the inability to gauge the company's reserve position from financial statements alone. Some form of disclosure is indicated—appropriately qualified where necessary to warn the reader of the many uncertainties involved in estimates of mineral reserves.

At the other extreme, some theorists argue that values expected to be realized in the future from additions to mineral reserves during the year should be reported in current financial statements. This alternative is based on the view that reserves discovered are resources arising from current operations. But it is doubtful whether the present worth of the future net revenue to be obtained from current discoveries can be estimated precisely enough to warrant representation to the investor that it has been or will be realized. Since quantities, ultimate sales prices, and recovery costs of mineral reserves may all be uncertain, the recording of revenue before the point of sale represents a departure from the realization convention that does not meet the criteria for departures discussed in Chapter 3.

Although the economist concerned with total national product may be justified in viewing the discovery of usable mineral reserves as an increase in resources and values, a corporation must produce and sell the minerals before it can produce a return on capital in a form distributable to investors. There should be a reasonably high probability that disposable income will become available in the foreseeable future before it is reported to the investor as having been earned. Before minerals are extracted and sold, the requisite degree of probability for recognizing revenue does not exist in extractive industries, since the realizable amounts remain uncertain until the point of sale is reached.

The conclusion that revenue should be recognized only at the point of sale does not deny, however, the crucial importance of the discovery of mineral deposits in extractive industries. The conclusion is reasonable because of the high degree of uncertainty found in extractive industries, but the problem of giving appropriate recognition to the crucial event of mineral discovery must still be solved.

An alternative to reporting realized income when mineral reserves are increased by discovery or development is suggested by W. A. Paton and A. C. Littleton who support departure from the cost basis in these and similar circumstances but suggest that an unrealized income account be credited:

> At times, resources are discovered or developed which have an immediate economic significance far in excess of the actual outlay required for their acquisition. In the field of natural resource exploitation, for example, an important oil pool may be discovered by exploratory work at a nominal outlay. Similarly a device or process of considerable market value may be developed and patented without an expenditure at all commensurate with such value. In extreme situations of this type it may be necessary to establish formally a new point of departure on the basis of implied cash cost—the amount of money which would unquestionably be necessary to acquire the resource in its established commercial status—in lieu of an actual bargained-price. There is no warrant in this suggestion, it should be emphasized, for writing up assets to new levels on the basis of mere hopes and expectations, or for opening the records to estimates not supported by conclusive evidence. It is purely a question of establishing a dependable starting point for resources having a clear-cut commercial value that have been acquired under extraordinary conditions.
>
> It is hardly necessary to say that the acquisition of property through donation or discovery does not create an earned surplus.[2]

Even this modification in recording discovery values has several shortcomings, including: (1) the uncertainties in extractive industries that make the estimates of value unreliable, (2) the confusion to statement users that might result from the appearance on the balance sheet of an unusual account (unrealized income), and (3) the fact that for the sake of consistency it would also be necessary to estimate the uncertain amount of future costs associated with the unrealized income.

A reasonable compromise, making the best of a difficult situation, would be to supplement financial statements with data on mineral reserve quantities and operating activities. The data should be appropriately qualified by indicating the limitations of measurement techniques and economic recovery factors, so as to caution the users of the financial statements against attributing greater accuracy and significance to the data than is warranted.

Relevant data would include the total quantity of reserves owned and the quantity added during the year (whether by discovery, by

---

[2] *An Introduction to Corporate Accounting Standards*, 1940, pp. 28-29.

development, or by revision of estimate). Undoubtedly, in most industries it would be useful to state separately mineral reserves which can be produced from existing facilities and mineral reserves which are yet to be developed.

Other relevant data might include: undeveloped acreage and claims; changes in these assets during the period; an indication of the magnitude of exploration and development operations in physical terms such as the number of wells and cores or feet of shaft drilled and the amount (tons) of overburden removed; and production data regarding quantities of minerals produced and sold, quantities of total rock mined, and so forth. If anticipated rates of extraction are reasonably predictable, that information might also be useful. To the extent that it is practicable, data on reserves and undeveloped properties should be presented in appropriate geographical and other classifications that may be significant in assessing their potential usefulness.

Short-term effects can disguise long-term trends unless data are given for a relatively long period of years. Mineral reserve data for individual years or for only a few years are not very significant because many years are usually involved both in realizing profits from mineral reserves and properties and in assessing the cumulative effects of expenditures. Comparative data for a period of time corresponding to the typical cycle from exploration to production should be given (say 10 to 20 years). The intent of disclosing reserve and operating data should be to indicate the pattern of physical effort and achievement as an aid to interpretation of current financial reports.

Present Practices Regarding Disclosure of Mineral Reserves and Operating Activities. Table 3, page 142, shows the incidence of disclosure of selected indicators of physical activity and results in the 265 annual reports to stockholders.

Physical data were usually presented in comparative form; five- to ten-year periods were common but two nonferrous metal producers gave up to 25 years of comparative data. Most of the 52 oil companies which reported number of wells drilled listed the number of producing oil wells, producing gas wells, and dry holes completed during the year. Petroleum companies which gave reserve estimates usually did not show gas separately. Some companies presented physical data for selected parts of their operations. One nonintegrated petroleum company disclosed the estimated reserves of oil in one field and the estimated recoverable reserves in oil shale. A nonferrous metal company expressed reserve data in terms of estimated remaining years of

TABLE 3

Frequency of Presentation of Physical Operating Data in Annual Reports to Stockholders

Item	Integrated Petroleum	Nonintegrated Petroleum	Iron	Nonferrous Metal	Coal	Bauxite, Asbestos, and Uranium	Salt, Sulfur, and Potash	Cement, Stone, Gravel, and Sand
Total number of reports reviewed	54	56	25	61	18	10	8	33
Production data:								
Quantity	45	43	12	54	14	6	4	2
Domestic and foreign shown separately	23	4	1	8	0	1	1	0
Domestic shown geographically	18	9	0	34	0	2	2	0
Reserve data:								
Estimated total	11	15	1	36	2	1	0	1
Change during year	9	10	0	20	2	1	0	0
Geographical distribution	1	0	0	14	0	1	0	0
Acreage:								
Total held	27	20	0	4	0	0	0	0
Change during year	29	5	0	3	0	0	1	0
Geographical distribution	17	3	0	4	0	0	0	0
Undeveloped shown separately	18	17	0	3	0	0	0	0
Other information on mining activities:								
Wells drilled, core drilling, feet of shafts and crosscuts, overburden removed, etc.	26	26	1	29	2	2	3	0
Producing wells owned	20	24	N.A.	N.A.	N.A.	N.A.	0	N.A.
Discussion of exploration and/or development activities	20	21	4	53	8	3	1	6

production held in reserves rather than in quantities of minerals. Two other nonferrous metal companies indicated estimated recoverable reserves in selected mines.

The Form 10-K reports and prospectuses were also examined to determine the nature and amount of disclosure. Based on the sample of 69 companies, about the same degree of disclosure was included in the reports to the Securities and Exchange Commission as in the annual reports to stockholders. In some respects the Form 10-K contained less information than the annual reports. Form 10-K was substantially more informative only in the area of property account details and depletion, depreciation, and amortization practices. On the other hand, Form 10-K lacks the narrative description and accompanying physical data on operations to be found in annual reports to stockholders. Prospectuses are more informative than Form 10-K and some reports to stockholders in this respect since they must contain mineral reserve data.

Classification of Financial Accounts

Extractive operations entail a series of processes culminating in the sale of minerals: discovery, development, and production. Although all three processes are necessary to the final result, each is largely distinctive and the emphasis on any one process can vary substantially without immediately affecting the level of activity in the other two. This feature of multiple, largely independent processes sets extractive operations apart from most manufacturing operations which involve either a single process or a group of closely integrated processes requiring careful coordination of relative effort to produce the desired quantity of goods.

Recommended Practice. When full correlation of effort and result is obtainable from financial statements, as in manufacturing operations, disclosure of expenditures in each process is perhaps not significant. In extractive operations, in which correlation of effort and result from financial statements is obscured by the presence of "off balance sheet" assets, disclosure of expenditures in each process, especially the discovery process, takes on added importance. Therefore it is recommended that:

> **Recommendation 18.** *Financial data should be classified by function to facilitate correlation with mineral reserve and operating statistics.*

Functional classifications in both the property accounts and the income statement are more easily related to changes in mineral reserves than are classifications by nature of the expense which cut across functional lines.

The properties section of the balance sheet should include the following accounts, each of which contains a class of expenditure distinctive from the others, either in the degree of association with known mineral reserves or in estimated useful life.[3]

> Properties and mineral rights
> Undeveloped mineral properties and rights, less
>   accumulated provision for loss of $_____ $_____
> Producing mineral properties and rights, less accumulated depletion of $_____   _____
> Deferred development costs, less accumulated
>   amortization of $_____   _____

It would be desirable to classify expenses pertaining to the extractive operations so as to distinguish development and exploration costs charged to income from production costs and to show cash exploration costs and write-offs or amortization of undeveloped property costs separately. Depletion, depreciation, and amortization of capitalized property costs should also be shown apart from functional cost classifications in the income statement, and the amount of depletion should preferably be set out separately. Thus, the following expense details should be shown:

> Production expenses
> Exploration costs
> Development costs
> Amortization and write-off of
>   undeveloped properties
> Depletion
> Depreciation and amortization

These suggested expense accounts would indicate the magnitude of expenditures in each of the various phases of operations, and would facilitate interpreting the physical results shown by reserve and other operating statistics.

---

[3] If the suggested details would result in cumbersome financial statements (as they might, for example, in a vertically integrated company), they could be furnished in supplementary tabulations.

Present Practice Regarding Classification of Financial Accounts. Twenty-two percent of the companies reviewed did not distinguish between the capitalized costs of mineral reserves and other capitalized costs such as land, buildings, and depreciable equipment. A majority, however, provided descriptive analyses ranging from two captions—such as (a) mining properties and claims and (b) plant and equipment—through a variety of six or more classifications. One petroleum company, for example, showed: leaseholds and mineral rights, intangible drilling costs, lease and well equipment, undeveloped leaseholds and mineral rights, other lands in fee, and other fixed assets. In general, the petroleum companies reported a greater number of property captions than the companies in the other extractive industries. Most of the nonpetroleum companies separated capitalized acquisition costs of mineral properties ("mining claims," "coal land," "leaseholds and mineral rights") from other capital items such as equipment and development costs. Several of these companies, however, did not distinguish producing from unproven properties.

Thirty-three of the integrated petroleum companies presented a functional classification of property accounts such as (a) exploration, (b) production, (c) refining, (d) transportation, (e) marketing, and (f) miscellaneous. None of the other companies presented a similar classification. Generalizations on disclosure of property account details in the 265 annual reports are presented in Table 4 on page 146. The broad categories shown contain a great variety of individual detail.

Almost all reports showed the total amount of accumulated depletion, depreciation, and amortization, but only 11 companies reported accumulated depletion of acquisition cost of mining properties separately.

Deferred development, preoperating, or stripping costs were reported by several companies, particularly nonferrous metal companies. The two iron ore companies carrying deferred development charges showed the accumulated amount of amortization separately; no other company disclosed the amount of accumulated amortization. Some indicated that the asset was carried net but did not state the amount of accumulated amortization. Since in some cases these deferred cost balances are grouped with property accounts, the accumulated amortization may have been included in the single amount of accumulated depletion, depreciation, and amortization.

Several reports contained a geographical breakdown of properties. One small nonintegrated producer, for example, showed lease and well investments in separate fields and horizons. More common prac-

TABLE 4

Disclosure of Property Account Details in Annual Reports to Stockholders

	Total	One Caption Only	Detail by Function	Detail by Descriptive Account
Integrated petroleum	54	10	33	11
Nonintegrated petroleum	56	6	—	50
Iron	25	8	—	17
Nonferrous metal	61	13	—	48
Coal	18	3	—	15
Bauxite, asbestos, and uranium	10	3	—	7
Salt, sulfur, and potash	8	3	—	5
Cement, stone, gravel, and sand	33	13	—	20
	265	59	33	173

tice was to give a breakdown between foreign and domestic assets with further geographical detail on domestic assets.

Development costs charged directly to operations are reported with dry-hole and other exploration costs by petroleum companies and with production costs by other mining companies. To the extent that development costs have been capitalized or deferred in successful undertakings, the charge to operations is included with depreciation and amortization. Thirty integrated and 27 nonintegrated petroleum companies showed separate amounts for dry-hole costs which presumably contained both exploratory and development unproductive drilling costs.

Only 2 of the 265 income statements examined showed separate amounts for amortization of undeveloped property costs. Both companies were nonintegrated petroleum producers. Since a much larger percentage of companies are known to amortize undeveloped property costs, at least in the petroleum industry, other companies presumably include similar amounts elsewhere, probably in exploration cost.

Depletion, depreciation, and amortization charges to income were set out in almost all reports reviewed but in the majority of reports as one amount. The following tabulation shows the number of companies in each category of primary activity that reported separately the amount of depletion.

	Number of Companies	
	Total	Disclosing Depletion*
Integrated petroleum	54	6
Nonintegrated petroleum	56	6
Iron	25	—
Nonferrous metal	61	9
Coal	18	5
Bauxite, asbestos, and uranium	10	1
Salt, sulfur, and potash	8	1
Cement, stone, gravel, and sand	33	2
	265	30

* Note, however, that 27 of the nonferrous and 2 of the cement, stone, gravel, and sand reports state or imply that no depletion is recorded as a matter of policy. Probably other companies adhere to the same policy without disclosure.

Presentation of Total Capital Program Expenditures

The relationship between financial statements and supplementary data on mineral reserves and operating activities would be comprehended more easily if a tabulation showing total capital program expenditures were provided. Some companies have already recognized that the usual source and disposition of funds statement does not fit the particular needs of extractive company reports and have modified funds statements to include unsuccessful drilling costs as a disposition of funds. Thus, dry-hole costs are added back to net income in determining total funds available, and the same amount is included in funds applied to capital expenditures.

The following recommendation would provide a medium for bringing together all expenditures in each critical function, regardless of whether capitalized or charged to expense:

> **Recommendation 19.** *A tabulation of exploration, acquisition, and development program expenditures combining both capital and expense items should be presented.*

The suggested tabulation would provide a bridge between total dollar effort reflected in the financial statements and results in physical terms reflected in supplementary data on mineral reserves and physical operating activities. Details in the capital program tabulation should set out total expenditures for each of the following activities separately:

> Exploration (including charges to income)
> Acquisition of undeveloped properties
> Development of proven mineral properties
> (including charges to income)

A separate tabulation as a vehicle for presentation of total expenditures of a capital nature, regardless of whether successful or unsuccessful, has apparent advantages. It provides a means of identifying the magnitude of effort with result, as expressed in both financial and statistical terms in balance sheet, income statement, and supplementary statistical data on mineral reserves and operating activities.

On the other hand, it must be acknowledged that any attempt to correlate discovery and development expenditures with mineral reserve data is seriously restricted by the uncertain relationships between expenditures and discoveries extending over a relatively long period of time. Precise correlation between annual expenditures and annual reserves discovered, or developed, is impossible and that goal is not sought by this recommendation for presentation of total discovery and development program expenditures.

At best, data on total discovery and development expenditures and on changes in mineral reserves can be used by the investor only as general indicators of the direction in which the company is going. For that purpose, the information given would be more meaningful to a company whose activity is exploration and production than to a vertically integrated company.

9

Summary

Considerations Underlying Recommendations

The characteristics of extractive operations create especially difficult accounting and reporting problems. Extractive industries require a substantial amount of capital which is exposed to a relatively high degree of risk and uncertainty through all phases of extractive operations. The degree of risk and uncertainty varies in the different phases of operations. Accordingly, accounting and reporting problems have been analyzed in terms of five operational phases: (1) prospecting, (2) acquisition, (3) exploration, (4) development, and (5) production.

The distinctive features of extractive operations as well as the investor's need for sufficient financial information to evaluate the risks which attach to his investment play a particularly significant role in defining the accounting and reporting problems peculiar to extractive industries. This study therefore analyzes the common accounting and reporting problems inherent in the singular objective of finding economically recoverable minerals to develop a central concept of reporting for the risks and results of attempting to achieve that objective. In the course of that analysis, the basic concepts and principles of general accounting theory especially applicable to extractive operations are considered. These include the cost basis for financial statements, the realization and matching conventions, and the concept of conservatism.

This study concludes that the common accounting problems of the extractive industries are best solved by adherence to the traditional concepts of realization and matching, tempered because of the risks involved by the concept of conservatism. The key to the application of the traditional concepts of realization and matching to extractive operations is found in the similarity of minerals in the ground to inventories. From this basic orientation, the study recommends accounting practices which, if adopted, would narrow alternative accounting practices in the extractive industries to those which differ only because the essential circumstances differ. Also, the study recommends accounting practices to cope with unique problems in accounting for special revenue transactions, and federal income taxes and financial reporting practices to achieve "full and fair disclosure" in financial reports.

The Capital/Expense Decision

Consideration of common accounting problems in the extractive industries involved in the capital/expense decision (Chapter 4) led to seven recommendations, as follows:

Recommendation 1. *The individual mineral deposit should be chosen as the cost center by which to identify costs with specific minerals-in-place.*

Recommendation 2. *Neither the medium of expenditure (company's own force vs. contract) nor the nature of the expenditure (intangible vs. tangible) should affect the amount of cost otherwise properly associated with minerals-in-place and capitalized.*

Recommendation 3. *Expenditures for prospecting costs, indirect acquisition costs, and most carrying costs should be charged to expense when incurred as a part of the current cost of exploration.*

Recommendation 4. *Direct acquisition costs of unproven properties should be capitalized and the estimated loss portion should be amortized to expense on a systematic and rational basis as part of the current cost of exploration.*

Recommendation 5. *Unsuccessful exploration and development expenditures should be charged to operations even though incurred on property units where commercially recoverable reserves exist.*

Recommendation 6. *The cost of gas and other hydrocarbons purchased to repressurize reservoirs should be recorded as an expense of the periods which receive the most benefit. Ordinarily, the cost should be charged to the period of reinjecting the hydrocarbons, but if a measurable and significant amount of revenue is ex-*

pected to result from the sale of the reinjected hydrocarbons, the cost should be deferred and matched with that revenue. In the latter situation, appropriate provision should be made for any loss because of nonrecoverability of a portion of the volumes injected.

Recommendation 7. *The estimated cost of restoring mined properties should be accrued ratably as minerals are produced.*

Disposition of Capitalized Costs

The discussion of the problems involved in the disposition of capitalized costs (Chapter 5) resulted in the following recommendations:

> **Recommendation 8.** *The current cost of exploration charged to expense should include a charge for the amortization of that portion of acquisition costs which will probably never be directly identified with minerals-in-place.*
>
> **Recommendation 9.** *Capitalized costs associated with minerals-in-place should be amortized ratably as the related minerals are extracted but may be amortized on the basis of time when time is the controlling factor in consumption of economic usefulness.*

Application of the latter recommendation requires attention to (1) definition of the total reserve quantity benefited, (2) allocation of total costs among joint-product minerals, and (3) selection of the appropriate stage in the extractive operations to measure exhaustion of capitalized costs. Difficult problems arise in the identification of particular costs with reserve quantity benefited, particularly the identification of development costs. The study recommends that development costs in all cases should be related to the number of mineral units made available through the expenditures.

The allocation of total cost to joint-product minerals is also a difficult problem. The study recommends amortization on the basis of an aggregation of joint-product mineral reserves using a reasonable common denominator to amortize capitalized costs at the rate of production of the combined units. Using relative market prices of the products is often as reasonable a method of aggregation as can be devised in the circumstances.

The study considers the question of whether production or sale is the more appropriate point at which to record amortization of capitalized mining cost and recommends that if stockpiled inventories are material and realization through sale is probable, a proportionate share of capitalized deferred mining cost should be included in inventories by recording depletion, depreciation, and amortization at the time of production.

Special attention is also given to the problem of depletion of nonferrous metal mines. The study recommends that the property cost associated with nonferrous metal mines should be charged to operations over the period during which the minerals are produced on the basis of the best estimate of an appropriate depletion rate.

Accounting for Revenue, Special Conveyances, and Joint Operations

Extractive operations give rise to many complicated contractual arrangements involving special conveyances of mineral rights and joint operations. Special accounting problems arising from these arrangements were considered in Chapter 6 and recommendations in this area are:

Recommendation 10. *Sales of a limited, partial interest in minerals-in-place (carved-out production payments) should be recorded as revenue in the periods during which the minerals are produced.*

Recommendation 11. *The deferred portion of proceeds from sales of carved-out production payments should be classified as noncurrent unearned revenue.*

Recommendation 12. *Amounts collected under take-or-pay contracts in excess of current deliveries should be recorded as unearned revenue unless circumstances indicate that the purchaser will not take delivery in future periods.*

Recommendation 13. *Amounts collected under temporary contractual gas prices subject to refund should be recorded as revenue of the current period only to the extent that refund is unlikely.*

Recommendation 14. *The capitalized acquisition costs associated with minerals-in-place should include the cost of commitments as well as the amount of cash paid outright. In ABC transactions, the estimated production costs rather than the face amount of the retained mineral payment should be included*

Recommendation 15. *Sales of continuing fractional interests in mineral properties for cash should be recorded as revenue and a proportionate share of property costs should be charged against revenue so that the net gain or loss is reflected in income.*

Accounting for Federal Income Taxes

Tax laws and regulations recognize the unusual features of extractive operations and create differences in book and tax income peculiar to extractive operations. Chapter 7 analyzed these differences to determine whether *APB Opinion 11*, "Accounting for Income Taxes," requires that interperiod income tax allocation be applied to the tax effect of the differences. The study finds nine important sources of differences between book and tax income of which two are wholly permanent and require no tax allocation, two are wholly temporary and require allocation of tax effect, and five are hybrid (part permanent and part temporary) and require allocation of the tax effect of the timing difference only.

The sources of difference listed according to recommended treatment are as follows:

Permanent (no tax allocation)
  Percentage depletion
  Intangible drilling and development costs

Temporary (allocate tax effect)
  Lifting costs capitalized in connection with ABC transactions
  Amortization of undeveloped property costs

Hybrid (allocate tax effect of timing difference only)
  Geological and geophysical costs directly related to acquisition of property
  Successful exploration and development costs of mineral properties other than oil and gas
  Revenue from sale of carved-out production payments to maximize allowable percentage depletion
  Revenue from take-or-pay contracts
  Revenue from gas contract price increases subject to approval

Recommended Presentation and Disclosure Practices

Particularly critical in the extractive industries is the amount and method of disclosure of information in financial statements. The study finds that present disclosure practices are inadequate and that conventional balance sheets and income statements standing alone or even with typical notes do not present fully the financial affairs of companies in the extractive industries. The conclusion in Chapter 8 is that extractive industries require a more comprehensive reporting medium and the following recommendations are developed:

> **Recommendation 16.** *A description of major accounting policies and practices should be included in notes to financial statements or in a supplement readily available to investors.*
>
> **Recommendation 17.** *Mineral reserves and operating activities should be sufficiently disclosed to facilitate evaluation of effort and result.*
>
> **Recommendation 18.** *Financial data should be classified by function to facilitate correlation with mineral reserve and operating statistics.*
>
> **Recommendation 19.** *A tabulation of exploration, acquisition, and development program expenditures combining both capital and expense items should be presented.*

* * * * * * *

The conclusions and recommendations of this study are summarized in this chapter without the supporting reasons. The analyses in Chapters 2 to 8 which support the decisions that certain practices are preferable and others unacceptable must be examined to judge the conclusions and recommendations.

Comments by Members of Project Advisory Committee

Comments of Gordon T. Bethune

Mr. Bethune feels that the firm recommendations in Chapter 8 regarding the extent of supplementary information on mineral reserves, exploration and production activities and related capital programs, are not practical and not meaningful to the investor in light of the many qualifications attaching to the data. In an enterprise where the major business is the extraction or sale of minerals, appropriate general information should be supplied as to development, reserves and production; however, the type of detail recommended, particularly in the case of integrated enterprises where the raw material extraction is primarily a part of the production process, is not appropriate to the evaluation of the business by the investor and can be detrimental to the competitive position of his company.

Comments of R. Hersel Hughes, Richard M. McGowen, and Charles W. Plum

Full Cost Accounting

We are in full agreement with the author's conclusions, as related to the capital/expense decision, that full cost accounting may not result in fair reporting to the investor because it can be used to obscure adverse results.

Recommendation 1 (Cost Center)

We do not agree with the recommendation that the individual mineral deposit should be the cost center for the important oil and gas segment of the extractive industries. It is true that the discovery and exploitation of a mineral deposit is the purpose for which funds are spent. Therefore, the matching of expenditures with reserves is a theoretically sound aim. However, it has not been demonstrated that the benefits derived from the accumulation of costs in the mineral deposit cost center will improve financial reporting or the comparability in financial reporting. Nor has it been shown that the benefits from the designation of the mineral deposit as the cost center will compensate for the practical problems which will be created. For example, joint operations are common in the oil and gas industry. There is a legal obligation to accumulate costs, invoice joint owners, and report to these joint owners on a lease by lease basis. The lease is the logical managerial control unit for both exploration and production efforts, and control reports are tailored to fit this requirement. The lease is the basis for the assessment of all taxes, including ad valorem, severance, production, and federal income. Therefore, the lease, which has been generally accepted as the cost center in the oil industry for many years, is the logical unit to be used for cost accumulation purposes. This area is one in which comparability is already attained.

The study recognizes that if the other study recommendations are followed, the capital/expense decision is little affected by the cost center. Amortization of capitalized cost on the basis of production and mineral reserves would not be expected to be the same using different cost centers; but in our opinion, the use of fields rather than leases would not result in significantly different amortization expense. When it is further recognized that these amortization charges are based on mineral reserve estimates subject to substantial revision, we doubt that any perceptible improvement in comparability of data and financial reporting would result if all companies used field cost centers rather than leases.

Recommendation 3 (Geological and Geophysical Costs)

The difficulty in properly associating the total amount of geological and geophysical costs with minerals-in-place cannot be denied. Even though the total amount cannot be associated, this does not appear to justify expensing those costs that can be identified and associated.

We agree that geological and geophysical costs eventually capitalized as producing property costs may not be material for all companies; however, if material, we believe that portion of such costs which can be identified and associated with minerals-in-place should be capitalized.

Since both prospecting costs and acquisition costs are essentially exploratory in nature, it is logical that acquisition costs and prospecting costs which can be associated with the acquisitions should be afforded the same handling. In our opinion, it would be more appropriate to capitalize and amortize both acquisition and associated prospecting costs which can be positively identified with the acquisition and retention of mineral properties.

Recommendation 18 (Correlation of Financial Data with Mineral Reserves)

We believe that the correlation of expenditures with mineral reserves found and developed is highly impractical, if not impossible. There is no practical way to separate development expenditures from expenditures which may be capitalized that result from normal operations or technological improvements, such as secondary recovery. The time lag between initial exploration and the commencement of production for oil and gas properties is well known. There is little or no relationship between exploratory funds spent and reserves discovered in any one year. Initial production from a mineral deposit may not commence for two to five years after exploration has been concluded. Full development of a property may very well be done over a period of from twenty to forty years. During this time, engineers' estimates of recoverable reserves will be adjusted and revised many times as more definitive boundaries of reservoirs and reservoir performance are obtained. Therefore, the attempt to relate expenditures to reserves discovered and developed would, in our opinion, not only be misleading to the investor but would contribute nothing to financial reporting or the comparability of financial statements of oil and gas companies.

APPENDIX A

Mineral Production in the United States, 1963-1966

Source: U. S. Department of the Interior, Bureau of Mines, *Minerals Yearbook, 1966*, Vols. I-II (Metals, Minerals, and Fuels), 1967, pp. 106-108.

Mineral Production in the United States, 1963-1966

PRODUCTION[1]

Mineral	1963 Quantity	1963 Value (thousands)	1964 Quantity	1964 Value (thousands)	1965 Quantity	1965 Value (thousands)	1966 Quantity	1966 Value (thousands)
Mineral fuels:								
Asphalt and related bitumens (native):								
Bituminous limestone and sandstone and gilsonite .... short tons	1,632,645	$8,383	1,935,344	$10,038	1,911,664	$9,461	2,041,271	$8,438
Carbon dioxide, natural (estimate) thousand cubic feet	1,295,545	178	1,232,816	166	1,173,676	152	1,140,907	153
Coal:								
Bituminous and lignite[2] ...... thousand short tons	458,928	2,013,309	486,998	2,165,582	512,088	2,276,022	533,881	2,421,293
Pennsylvania anthracite .... do	18,267	153,503	17,184	148,648	14,866	122,021	12,941	100,663
Helium:								
Crude .... thousand cubic feet	1,420,300	15,147	3,197,016	35,322	3,566,734	39,848	3,654,700	41,556
Grade A .... do	809,100	28,318	830,481	25,923	819,100	28,880	951,400	32,541
Natural gas .... million cubic feet	14,746,663	2,328,030	r15,462,138	2,387,689	16,039,753	2,494,542	r17,232,134	r2,721,875
Natural gas liquids:								
Natural gasoline and cycle products thousand gallons	6,534,967	439,173	7,000,181	463,600	7,288,070	494,354	7,548,428	520,635
LP gases .... do	10,302,250	359,770	10,743,591	362,792	11,257,267	417,249	12,134,294	527,223
Peat .... short tons	546,621	5,423	639,690	6,198	603,746	6,080	505,858	6,501
Petroleum (crude) .... thousand 42-gallon barrels	2,752,723	7,965,743	2,786,822	8,017,078	r2,848,462	r8,158,150	3,028,084	r8,727,387
Total mineral fuels	XX	r13,317,000	XX	13,623,000	XX	r14,047,000	XX	15,108,000
Nonmetals (except fuels):								
Abrasive stone[4] .... short tons	2,693	255	3,186	292	3,603	432	3,806	515
Asbestos .... do	66,396	5,108	101,092	8,143	118,275	10,162	125,928	11,056
Barite .... thousand short tons	824	9,402	830	9,796	852	10,192	947	11,259
Boron minerals .... do	700	54,981	776	60,871	807	64,180	866	68,209
Bromine[5] .... thousand pounds	203,333	48,558	283,530	66,064	328,115	77,259	326,498	78,883
Calcite (optical grade) .... pounds	....	....	4	2	(6)	(6)	(6)	(6)

APPENDIX A: MINERAL PRODUCTION IN THE UNITED STATES, 1963-1966

		1963		1964		1965		1966	
Cement:									
Portland	thousand 376-pound barrels	342,036	1,095,884	358,378	1,145,108	366,802	1,154,448	373,091	1,162,984
Masonry	thousand 280-pound barrels	20,997	59,599	22,397	63,305	23,260	65,979	22,367	63,407
Natural and slag	thousand 376-pound barrels	352	1,407	283	1,057	279	1,027	233	872
Clays	thousand short tons	50,135	180,810	52,947	192,631	r 55,126	r 204,932	56,675	221,457
Emery	short tons	6,732	119	9,214	172	10,720	204	11,102	210
Feldspar	long tons	548,954	5,524	587,194	5,389	624,598	6,263	685,592	7,192
Fluorspar	short tons	199,948	9,001	217,137	9,723	240,932	10,889	253,068	10,841
Garnet (abrasive)	do	14,626	1,412	16,123	1,622	19,330	1,717	21,952	2,092
Gem stones (estimate)		NA	1,421	NA	1,474	NA	2,218	NA	2,437
Gypsum	thousand short tons	10,388	38,138	10,684	38,874	r 10,033	r 37,375	9,647	35,681
Lime	do	14,521	199,389	16,089	223,149	16,794	232,939	18,057	239,588
Magnesium compounds from sea water and brine (except for metals) short tons, MgO equivalent		520,699	39,323	599,698	42,177	r 637,857	r 47,197	650,300	46,610
Mica:									
Scrap	short tons	109,323	2,776	114,729	3,353	120,255	3,468	113,133	3,733
Sheet	pounds	102,961	13	242,662	58	716,086	185	4,500	1
Perlite	short tons	325,132	2,727	349,867	3,073	392,384	3,352	404,160	3,907
Phosphate rock	thousand short tons	22,238	139,861	25,715	161,067	r 29,482	r 193,323	39,050	261,121
Potassium salts	thousand short tons, K₂O equivalent	2,864	110,164	2,897	114,095	3,140	129,767	3,320	122,210
Pumice	thousand short tons	2,618	6,578	2,776	6,443	r 3,371	r 6,550	3,218	6,765
Pyrites	thousand long tons	825	5,698	847	5,471	875	5,333	873	5,088
Salt	thousand short tons	30,641	184,589	31,623	200,706	34,687	215,699	36,463	229,985
Sand and gravel	do	821,850	847,272	868,208	893,375	908,049	957,416	934,481	984,982
Sodium carbonate (natural)	short tons	1,119,081	27,616	1,274,745	30,451	1,494,105	34,717	1,737,511	40,674
Sodium sulfate (natural)	do	435,257	8,392	575,033	10,989	619,752	11,024	640,329	11,271
Stone [7]	thousand short tons	688,366	1,068,108	725,583	1,134,564	r 780,242	r 1,203,831	813,374	1,260,715
Sulfur:									
Frasch process mines	thousand long tons	4,995	99,014	6,035	120,776	7,251	r 164,654	7,721	201,292
Other mines	long tons	1,371	15	794	8	2,852	11	557	5
Talc, soapstone, and pyrophyllite	short tons	804,358	5,505	889,949	6,218	862,875	6,343	895,045	6,479
Tripoli	do	66,635	266	64,613	268	71,138	381	66,163	328
Vermiculite	thousand short tons	226	3,572	226	3,613	249	4,460	262	4,954
Value of items that cannot be disclosed: Aplite, brucite, (1965-66), calcium-magnesium chloride, diatomite, graphite, iodine, kyanite, lithium minerals, magnesite, greensand marl, olivine, staurolite, wollastonite, and values indicated by footnote 6		XX	XX	XX	XX	XX	65,028	XX	69,911
Total nonmetals		XX	r 4,316,000	XX	4,623,000	XX	r 4,933,000	XX	5,177,000

161

Table continued on pages 162 and 163—see footnotes at end of table.

Mineral Production in the United States, 1963-1966 (Cont'd)

PRODUCTION[1]

Mineral	1963 Quantity	1963 Value (thousands)	1964 Quantity	1964 Value (thousands)	1965 Quantity	1965 Value (thousands)	1966 Quantity	1966 Value (thousands)
Metals:								
Antimony ore and concentrate short tons, antimony content	645	(8)	632	(8)	845	(8)	927	(8)
Bauxite ....thousand long tons, dried equivalent	1,525	$17,234	1,601	$17,875	1,654	$18,632	1,796	$20,095
Copper (recoverable content of ores, etc.)..short tons	1,213,166	747,310	1,246,780	812,901	1,351,734	957,028	1,429,152	1,033,850
Gold (recoverable content of ores, etc.)..troy ounces	1,454,010	50,889	1,456,308	50,971	1,705,190	59,682	1,803,420	63,119
Iron ore, usable (excluding byproduct iron sinter) thousand long tons, gross weight	73,564	678,181	84,300	802,331	r 84,079	r 801,388	90,404	854,134
Lead (recoverable content of ores, etc.)..short tons	253,369	54,727	286,010	74,935	301,147	93,959	327,368	98,964
Manganese ore (35 percent or more Mn) short tons, gross weight	10,622	(8)	26,058	(8)	29,258	(8)	14,406	(8)
Manganiferous ore (5 to 35 percent Mn) .....do	543,125	(8)	238,776	(8)	332,763	(8)	324,926	(8)
Mercury ....76-pound flasks	19,117	3,623	14,142	4,452	19,582	11,176	22,008	9,722
Molybdenum (content of concentrate) thousand pounds	65,839	91,096	65,097	97,121	77,310	120,801	91,670	144,327
Nickel (content of ore and concentrate) ..short tons	13,394	(8)	15,420	(8)	16,188	(8)	15,036	(8)
Silver (recoverable content of ores, etc.) thousand troy ounces	35,243	45,076	36,334	46,980	39,806	51,469	43,669	56,463
Tin (content of concentrate) ....long tons	(8)	(8)	65	185	47	126	97	265
Titanium concentrate:								
Ilmenite ....short tons, gross weight	890,071	16,529	1,003,997	19,178	948,832	18,058	868,436	17,608
Rutile ....do	11,311	1,262	10,547	1,016	(8)	(8)	(8)	(8)
Tungsten ore and concentrate short tons, 60 percent WO₃ basis	5,657	7,202	9,244	11,251	7,949	13,028	8,912	17,620
Uranium ore ....short tons	r 5,613,570	r 115,220	5,359,653	111,707	r 4,385,995	r 84,154	4,352,651	77,524
Vanadium (recoverable in ore and concentrate) short tons	3,862	13,788	4,362	13,061	5,226	18,284	5,166	22,210

APPENDIX A: MINERAL PRODUCTION IN THE UNITED STATES, 1963-1966

Zinc (recoverable content of ores, etc.)..short tons	529,254	122,533	574,858	156,308	611,153	178,284	572,558	166,044
Value of items that cannot be disclosed: Beryllium concentrate, cobalt, magnesium chloride for magnesium metal, manganiferous residuum, platinum-group metals (crude), rare-earth metal concentrates, zirconium concentrate, and values indicated by footnote 8	XX	36,827	XX	40,183	XX	r 44,804	XX	39,117
Total metals	XX	2,002,000	XX	2,261,000	XX	r 2,471,000	XX	2,621,000
Grand total mineral production	XX	r 19,636,000	XX	20,507,000	XX	r 21,451,000	XX	22,906,000

---

r Revised.   NA Not available.   XX Not applicable.
[1] Production as measured by mine shipments, sales, or marketable production (including consumption by producers).
[2] Includes small quantity of anthracite mined in States other than Pennsylvania.
[3] Final figure; superseded figure given in commodity section.
[4] Grindstones, pulpstones, millstones (weight not recorded), grinding pebbles, sharpening stones, and tube-mill liners.
[5] Bromine content 1963, gross weight 1964-66.
[6] Figure withheld to avoid disclosing individual company confidential data; value included with "Nonmetal items that cannot be disclosed."
[7] Excludes abrasive stone, bituminous limestone, bituminous sandstone, and ground soapstone, all included elsewhere in table.
[8] Figure withheld to avoid disclosing individual company confidential data; value included with "Metal items that cannot be disclosed."

163

APPENDIX B

Excerpts from "Depletion Allowances for Mineral Production Reported on U.S. Tax Returns"*

COMPUTATION OF THE DEPLETION ALLOWANCE

Taxpayers compute depletion allowances using two different methods, cost depletion and percentage depletion, and take the higher of the two. However, exceptions are made in the case of . . . coal royalties if the capital gains option is elected—where the only method available is cost depletion. . . . Under the provisions of sections 631(c) and 1231 of the Code, lessors of coal properties held for more than six months prior to disposal may elect capital gains treatment for the difference between the sales price or royalty receipts and the adjusted basis of the coal, this basis being generally equivalent to the cost depletion sustained.

Cost depletion

Cost depletion may be likened to depreciation determined by the units-of-production method in that it is computed with reference to the cost of the property and the number of mineral units yielded by the property. Unit cost depletion is first determined by dividing the cost of the property (more technically, the adjusted basis of the property), by the total number of mineral units remaining. Total cost depletion is then basically the product of unit cost depletion and the number of minerals units actually sold. For example, if a mineral property cost $1,000,000 and contained an estimated 2,000,000 tons

---

*Source: U. S. Treasury Department, Internal Revenue Service, *Statistics of Income . . . 1960, Supplemental Report*, 1966.

of ore, unit cost depletion in the first year would amount to 50 cents. If 100,000 tons were sold in that year, total cost depletion would amount to $50,000. Assuming that the $50,000 cost depletion was higher than percentage depletion, in the next year the cost basis and mineral reserves would be adjusted downward, the number of units remaining would be 1,900,000 tons (2,000,000 − 100,000), and the unit cost depletion again 50 cents ($950,000 ÷ 1,900,000).

The basis of the property is adjusted downward by the amount of depletion claimed in the previous year whether determined under the cost or percentage method. If percentage depletion exceeded cost depletion in the first year, say $70,000, the adjusted basis would have been reduced to $930,000, and the unit cost depletion to 48.95 cents ($930,000 ÷ 1,900,000). Moreover, should the original estimate of 2,000,000 tons be revised, further adjustments to unit cost depletion would be made.

Percentage depletion

Percentage depletion differs from cost depletion in that it is determined solely with reference to income. It is computed by applying percentage rates, which vary according to mineral type, to gross income from mineral properties. The statutory percentage depletion rates are prescribed as 5, 10, 15, 23, and 27½ percent for different classes of minerals. Percentage depletion is computed on each separate property and, in every case, is limited to 50 percent of the net income on the property before depletion.

Gross income from mineral properties generally encompasses the receipts accruing from the mining or extraction process—i.e., prior to refining or subsequent manufacture. However, except in the case of oil or gas, gross income also includes the values added by certain treatment and transportation processes, considered to be within the scope of "mining." Consequently, the more treatment processes considered as mining, the greater is gross income, and in turn, percentage depletion. Amounts paid by operators or lessees to owners or lessors of mineral producing properties as royalties and bonuses are excluded from the gross income upon which the operators' percentage depletion is computed. These payments, on the other hand, constitute the gross income which the lessors use to compute percentage depletion.

Since percentage depletion is computed solely with reference to gross and net income, percentage depletion may be taken even though there is no longer any remaining cost basis and additional cost depletion is no longer possible. The computation of depletion being made on each separate property, a taxpayer may claim percentage depletion on some properties and cost depletion on others. Moreover, on some properties taxpayers may not be able to take the allowance if the accumulated depletion has reduced the adjusted basis of the property to zero, precluding cost depletion, while net losses on the property, through the 50 percent of the net income limitation, preclude percentage depletion.

Notwithstanding the requirement that depletion be computed on each separate property, certain aggregations of mineral deposits or wells into a single property for computing depletion are permitted. For example, mines within a single "operating unit" operated by common field or operating personnel may be aggregated. There are other factors which may also be taken to indicate that the mineral interests do in fact constitute an "operating unit," all characterized by the fact that they refer to a producing unit and not to an administrative or sales organization.

Effect of other expenses on depletion

In addition to depletion, nearly all expenses incurred in preparing properties for production may be deducted from gross income. The Internal Revenue Code also permits taxpayers to expense—i.e., deduct currently or ratably with production—certain outlays incurred in the exploration and development of mineral properties. As these costs are expensed, net income is lowered and owing to the 50 percent limitation, there may be a lowering effect on percentage depletion. Expensing of such costs, moreover, also results in a lower adjusted basis than if costs are capitalized and consequently, in lower cost depletion. However, inasmuch as the current deduction or expensing of outlays generally results in a greater reduction of taxable income, taxpayers seldom choose to capitalize those outlays for which an election to expense is permitted.

· · · · · · · · · · · · · · · ·

EXPLANATION OF TERMS

Allowable depletion, allowable percentage depletion, and allowable cost depletion

Percentage depletion on the property is determined by the lesser of (a) the statutory percentage rate on gross income from the property,

APPENDIX B: EXCERPTS FROM "DEPLETION ALLOWANCES FOR MINERAL PRODUCTION REPORTED ON U.S. TAX RETURNS"

or (b) fifty percent of net income from the property, before depletion. The cost depletion is limited to the adjusted basis depletion sustained. For each property, the "allowable" depletion is the higher of percentage or cost depletion. . . .

• • • • • • • • • • • • • • •

Deductions exclusive of depletion, total

This is the total of allowable deductions from gross income from mineral properties, from which are derived net income and the fifty percent of net income limitation. For purposes of this report, total deductions consist of the following: Exploration; development, including intangible drilling and development costs for oil and gas; dry holes on oil and gas properties; depreciation; operating expenses; taxes; and overhead and other. Also see: Deductions on nonproducing properties.

Deductions on nonproducing properties

Deductions on nonproducing properties include costs for exploration and development, abandonment losses, and dry-hole expenditures, on properties found unproductive, where the costs cannot be recovered through depletion. These deductions are permitted the taxpayer in computing the net income subject to tax although they are not used for purposes of computing the 50 percent of net income limitation.

These expenses are incurred as a result of geological and geophysical investigation, where these investigations do not lead to acquisition or retention of mineral properties or leasehold interests. They may also come about through the surrender of leases and royalties before their costs are recouped. The greater portion of these expenses are incurred in the search for oil and gas.

Excluded from these deductions, and other portions of the study, are expenditures pursuant to payments for exploration, development, and mining for national defense purposes under section 621 of the Code.

Depreciation

Depreciation is an allowance for the wear and tear of equipment. For equipment used in the extraction or mining process, depreciation is one of the expenses taken into consideration when computing net income for purposes of the 50 percent limitation. Those costs of exploration and development which are capitalized and involve purchases of depreciable assets are recovered through depreciation allowances.

Development expenses

These are expenses incurred during a specific taxable year for the development of a mine or other natural deposit, excluding expenditures for property subject to depreciation. Development expenditures, in contrast to exploration expenses, are those made after mineral deposits are shown to exist that would justify commercial exploitation. The expenditures may be deducted currently or deferred and deducted ratably with production.

As shown in this report for oil and gas properties, development expenses are "intangible" drilling and development costs (IDC) of oil and gas production. IDC include those costs associated with: Drilling, shooting, and cleaning wells; ground clearing, road making, surveying, and geological work to prepare for drilling; and other expenses necessary for drilling wells and preparing them for production. These costs are intangible in the sense that the expenditures do not result in an asset which could be sold or salvaged for another purpose. Taxpayers may choose to capitalize these costs in depletable and depreciable asset accounts but this option is seldom used.

Dry-hole costs for oil and gas

Taxpayers are permitted to expense dry-hole costs as incurred. If the dry holes are encountered on otherwise producing properties, the costs are included among those deductions from gross income which enter into the computation of the 50 percent of net income limitation on allowable percentage depletion. Dry-hole costs on nonproducing properties are included in the item, "Deductions on nonproducing properties"....

Taxpayers electing to capitalize intangible drilling costs may also capitalize dry-hole costs. This option is, in fact, seldom used by taxpayers.

Exploration expenses

Exploration expenses are incurred while ascertaining the existence, extent, location, and quality of mineral deposits, prior to the development stage of the mine or deposit. The deduction for exploration expenses allowed to the taxpayer may not exceed $100,000 in any one year with an overall lifetime limitation of $400,000. Exploration costs may be currently expensed or set up as deferred expenses and deducted ratably as the deposit is exhausted. Costs in excess of the limitation must be capitalized in depletable and depreciable asset accounts. [As an alternative, the taxpayer may elect to write off all exploration cost when incurred without regard to those dollar limitations, but the resulting deductions are subject to recapture after the mine enters the producing stage.]

The deduction for exploration expenses, incurred in the acquisition or retention of a mineral interest, is not allowed on oil and gas properties. These costs include but are not limited to expenses of geological and geophysical investigations. They must be capitalized and recovered through depletion unless the results are unsuccessful. If unsuccessful, they may be written off as losses when the property is found worthless and abandoned. These losses are included in the item "Deductions on nonproducing properties."

Fifty percent of net income before depletion

Allowable percentage depletion may not exceed 50 percent of the net income before depletion from the mineral property. This limitation is computed for each separate property. The limitation precludes the taking of percentage depletion for properties on which net losses have been sustained.

• • • • • • • • • • • • • • • •

Gross income from mineral properties

Gross income from mineral properties is the income before deductions from the sale of ores and minerals. Generally, gross income is equivalent to the representative market or field price at the mine or well, i.e., from the mining or extraction process. However, except in the case of oil and gas, gross income also includes certain treatment and transportation values added.

Minerals used in the manufacture of cement, e.g., limestone, and clays, were the subject of legislation in 1960 and 1961, partly retroactive in character. This legislation clarified the treatment processes considered as part of gross income. Some taxpayers' returns for 1960 reflected provisions of this legislation. In addition, the returns for which depletion information was obtained from the Treasury Depletion Survey showed amended tax information resulting from this legislation.

As used in this report, gross income for operating interests excludes royalties or other payments by the taxpayer to nonoperating interests. Royalties, and other payments if subject to depletion, constitute gross income for taxpayers with nonoperating interests. When nonoperating income was reported by the taxpayer along with operating income as part of the total receipts of a business, and the amounts were not allocated as to the type of interest, combined amounts were entered as gross income for operating interests. When two different types of minerals were reported on depletion schedules, each subject to a different percentage rate, and the depletion deduction or other deduction items could not be allocated among the different types of minerals, the information was entered under the applicable rate and mineral producing the largest gross income.

When computing gross income and the depletion allowance, the "property" is considered as each separate interest held by the taxpayer in each mineral deposit in each separate tract of land. Taxpayers, however, have been permitted to aggregate and form as a single property for tax purposes, mineral deposits and wells included in a single lease or acquisition, or which constitute a single "operating unit." An operating unit refers to a producing unit, and not to an administrative or sales organization. Mineral deposits or wells may be considered as part of an operating unit when they have common operating personnel, supply and maintenance facilities, processing or treatment plants, or storage facilities. Nonoperating interests may also be aggregated where the taxpayer shows he will sustain a hardship if the interests are not treated as one property.

Provisions of the Revenue Act of 1964, however, generally preclude taxpayers from combining an operating interest in oil and gas in one tract of land with a similar operating interest in another tract.

• • • • • • • • • • • • • • • •

Net income, or loss, before depletion

Net income, or loss, before depletion is defined as gross income from mineral properties less all allowable deductions except depletion. Where a net loss has been sustained on a property, whether that property is the result of an aggregation or not, the 50 percent of net income limitation precludes the taxpayers from taking percentage depletion for that property.

Nonoperating interests

Nonoperating interests are those held by taxpayers who receive income from royalties, production payments, net profits interests, and similar arrangements, but who have no obligation for the expenses of operating the property.

A royalty interest is a right, entitling the owner to a specified fraction, in kind or value, of the production from the property. A production payment provides the holder with a stipulated fraction of production for a limited period of time or until a specified sum or number of units of production has been received, which in any event must terminate before the economic life of the property. A net profits interest is similar to a royalty in that it is a share of production, but differs in that the share is measured by the net profits from the property. Nonoperators receiving income from these interests treat the amounts received as the gross income from mineral properties and compute depletion on these amounts.

However, the sale of royalties and "in-oil" payments (production payments are used primarily for oil and gas) are treated differently. Royalties are considered to represent a share of a capital asset; in-oil payments are an assignment of future income. The sale of a royalty can qualify for capital gains treatment but the sale of the in-oil payment does not qualify if the seller retains an interest in the property from which it was created. The differential treatment is given since royalties cover the life of the property; in-oil payments are limited in time, money, or barrels of crude, terminating before the economic life of the property. Sellers of in-oil payments which result in ordinary income sometimes treat the income arising from the sale in installments under section 453(b) of the Internal Revenue Code.

In many instances, holders of nonoperating interests may deplete for tax purposes lease bonus and advance royalty payments which they receive although no production has occurred to deplete the property in a physical sense. Generally, where it has become evident that no actual production is to take place and the lease is abandoned without production, depletion allowances must be restored to income in the year of abandonment.

• • • • • • • • • • • • • • • • • •

Operating interests

Operating interests, often called working interests, are held by those taxpayers who, in addition to receiving a share of income from mineral properties, are burdened with the obligations of development. Most commonly, these interests are created through a lease arrangement whereby the operator or lessee may pay the landowner or lessor a royalty, i.e., a share of production, a bonus, and annual rents or delay rentals until such time as the property is producing (and royalties paid) or the lease is abandoned. Operating interests, thus created, may be further burdened by the sale or reservation of royalties and production payments.

APPENDIX C

List of 265 Companies Whose 1964 Annual Reports Were Reviewed for Disclosure Practices

Integrated Petroleum

American Petrofina, Inc.
Apco Oil Corporation
Asamera Oil Corp., Ltd.
Ashland Oil & Refining Company
Associated Oil and Gas Company
The Atlantic Refining Company
Barber Oil Corporation
Billups Western Petroleum Company
The British American Oil Company Limited
Cabot Corporation
Canadian Delhi Oil, Ltd.
Canadian Petrofina Limited
Christiana Oil Corporation
Cities Service Company
Clark Oil & Refining Corporation
Coastal States Gas Producing Company
Continental Oil Company
Crown Central Petroleum Corporation
Empire State Oil Company
Frontier Refining Company
Getty Oil Company
Gulf Oil Corporation
Hess Oil & Chemical Corporation
Husky Oil Canada Ltd.
Imperial Oil Limited
Kendall Refining Company
Kerr-McGee Oil Industries, Inc.
Marathon Oil Company
McWood Corporation
Mohawk Petroleum Corporation

Murphy Oil Company Ltd.
Occidental Petroleum Corporation
Pacific Petroleums, Ltd.
Phillips Petroleum Company
The Pure Oil Company
Quaker State Oil Refining Corporation
Richfield Oil Corporation
The Shamrock Oil and Gas Corporation
Shell Oil Company
Signal Oil and Gas Company
Sinclair Oil Corporation
Sinclair Venezuelan Oil Company
Skelly Oil Company
Socony Mobil Oil Company, Inc.
Standard Oil Company of California
Standard Oil Company (Indiana)
Standard Oil Company (New Jersey)
The Standard Oil Company (Ohio)
Sun Oil Company
Texaco Canada Limited
Texaco Inc.
Tidewater Oil Company
Union Oil Company of California
The Wiser Oil Company

Nonintegrated Petroleum

Aberdeen Petroleum Corporation
Ambassador Oil Corporation
Amerada Petroleum Corporation
Aztec Oil & Gas Company
Banff Oil Ltd.

Barnwell Industries, Inc.
Belco Petroleum Corporation
Buttes Gas & Oil Co.
Camerina Petroleum Corporation
Central Del Rio Oils Limited
Consolidated Oil & Gas, Inc.
Devon-Palmer Oils Ltd.
Diversa, Inc.
Dixilyn Corporation
Dome Petroleum Limited
Dorchester Gas Producing Company
Eason Oil Company
Equity Oil Company
Falcon Seaboard Drilling Company
Fargo Oils Ltd.
Felmont Petroleum Corporation
General American Oil Company of Texas
Goff Oil Co.
Great Basins Petroleum Co.
Helmerich & Payne, Incorporated
Holly Oil Company
Home Oil Company Limited
Hugoton Plains Gas & Oil Company
International Oil & Gas Corporation
Intex Oil Company
The Jupiter Corporation
Kewanee Oil Company
Kin-Ark Oil Company
Kingwood Oil Company
Leonard Refineries, Inc.
The Louisiana Land and Exploration Company
Magna Oil Corporation
McCulloch Oil Corporation of California
Midwest Oil Corporation
Mission Corporation
Nortex Oil & Gas Corp.
Ocean Drilling & Exploration Company
Pauley Petroleum Inc.
Petroleum Exploration
Pubco Petroleum Corporation
Reserve Oil & Gas Company
Santa Fe Drilling Company
Savoy Industries, Incorporated

South Shore Oil and Development Company
The Superior Oil Company
Sunset International Petroleum Corporation
Texas Gas Producing Co.
Tex-Star Oil & Gas Corp.
Triad Oil Co., Ltd.
U. S. Natural Gas Corp.
Zapata Off-Shore Company

Iron

Alan Wood Steel Company
The Algoma Steel Corporation, Limited
Armco Steel Corporation
Bethlehem Steel Corporation
The Cleveland Cliffs Iron Company
The Colorado Fuel and Iron Corporation
Dominion Foundries and Steel, Limited
Dominion Steel and Coal Corporation, Limited
Great Northern Iron Ore Properties
The Hanna Mining Company
Inland Steel Company
Interlake Steel Corporation
Jones & Laughlin Steel Corporation
Koppers Company, Inc.
Lone Star Steel Company
McLouth Steel Corporation
National Steel Corporation
Pittsburgh Steel Company
Republic Steel Corporation
Sharon Steel Corporation
The Steel Company of Canada, Limited
Steep Rock Iron Mines Limited
United States Steel Corporation
Wheeling Steel Corporation
Woodward Iron Company

Nonferrous Metal

American Smelting and Refining Company

APPENDIX C: LIST OF 265 COMPANIES WHOSE 1964 ANNUAL
REPORTS WERE REVIEWED FOR DISCLOSURE PRACTICES

American Zinc, Lead and Smelting Company
The Anaconda Company
Atlantic Coast Copper Corporation Limited
Callahan Mining Corporation
Campbell Red Lake Mines Limited
Campbell Chibougamau Mines Ltd.
The Canadian Faraday Corporation Limited
Cerro Corporation
The Consolidated Mining and Smelting Company of Canada Limited
Copper Range Company
Cyprus Mines Corporation
Day Mines, Inc.
Denison Mines Limited
Dickenson Mines Limited
Discovery Mines Limited
Falconbridge Nickel Mines Limited
First Maritime Mining Corp. Limited
The Fresnillo Company
Giant Yellowknife Mines Limited
The Goldfield Corporation
Gunnar Mining Limited
Hecla Mining Company
Highland-Bell Limited
Hollinger Consolidated Gold Mines, Limited
Homestake Mining Company
Hudson Bay Mining and Smelting Co., Limited
Inspiration Consolidated Copper Company
International Mining Corporation
The International Nickel Company of Canada, Limited
Kerr Addison Mines Limited
Lake Shore Mines, Limited
Madsen Red Lake Gold Mines Limited
Magma Copper Company
Malartic Gold Fields Limited
Matthiessen & Hegeler Zinc Company
McIntyre Porcupine Mines Limited
Minerals & Chemicals Philipp Corporation
Molybdenum Corporation of America
National Lead Company
The New Jersey Zinc Company
New Park Mining Company
New York and Honduras Rosario Mining Company
Noranda Mines Limited
Phelps Dodge Corporation
Quemont Mining Corporation Limited
Rio Algom Mines Limited
Pacific Tin Consolidated Corporation
The Patino Mining Corporation
Placer Development, Limited
Shattuck Denn Mining Corporation
Sherritt Gordon Mines Limited
Silver Miller Mines, Limited
Stanrock Uranium Mines Limited
Sunshine Mining Company
The Susquehanna Corporation
United Keno Hill Mines Limited
United Park City Mines Company
United States Smelting, Refining and Mining Company
Wright-Hargreaves Mines, Limited
The Yukon Consolidated Gold Corporation Limited

Coal

Allegheny Ludlum Steel Corporation
Ayrshire Collieries Corporation
Consolidation Coal Company
The Crow's Nest Pass Coal Company, Limited
Dominion Coal Company, Limited
Glen Alden Corporation
Great West Coal Company, Limited
Island Creek Coal Company
Maust Coal & Coke Corporation
The North American Coal Corporation

Oglebay Norton Company
Peabody Coal Company
The Pittston Company
Rochester & Pittsburgh Coal Company
The Virginia Coal and Iron Company
Virginia Iron, Coal and Coke Co.
Westmoreland Coal Company
Zeigler Coal & Coke Company

Bauxite, Asbestos, and Uranium

Aluminum Company of America
Aluminium Limited
Asbestos Corporation, Limited
Cassiar Asbestos Corporation
Green Mountain Uranium Corporation
Kaiser Aluminum & Chemical Corporation
Reynolds Metals Company
Union Carbide Corporation
United Asbestos Corporation, Limited
Western Nuclear, Inc.

Salt, Sulfur, and Potash

Diamond Crystal Salt Company
Duval Corporation
Freeport Sulphur Company
Gulf Sulphur Corporation
International Salt Company
Pan American Sulphur Company
Potash Company of America
Texas Gulf Sulphur Company

Cement, Stone, Gravel, and Sand

Alpha Portland Cement Company
American Cement Corporation
Basic Incorporated
California Portland Cement Company
Canada Cement Company Limited
Dolese & Shepard Co.
Foote Mineral Company
General Portland Cement Company
Giant Portland Cement Company
Ideal Cement Company
Inland Cement Company Limited
Kaiser Cement & Gypsum Corporation
Keystone Portland Cement Company
LaFarge Cement of North America Ltd.
Lehigh Portland Cement Company
Limestone Products Corporation of America
Louisville Cement Company
Marquette Cement Manufacturing Company
Martin Marietta Corporation
Missouri Portland Cement Company
Medusa Portland Cement
Monolith Portland Cement Company
North Lily Mining Company
Ocean Cement & Supplies Ltd.
Oklahoma Cement Company
Oregon Portland Cement Company
Pacific Cement & Aggregates, Incorporated
Penn-Dixie Cement Corporation
Pennsylvania Glass Sand Corporation
St. Lawrence Cement Co.
Texas Industries, Inc.
Vulcan Materials Company
The Whitehall Cement Manufacturing Company

APPENDIX D

Glossary

ABC Transaction. An acquisition of mineral reserves involving three parties: seller, purchaser, and financier. In a typical ABC transaction, the seller receives cash from the purchaser and the financier in exchange for the mineral reserves, the purchaser receives the mineral reserves in exchange for cash to the seller and granting a production payment to be satisfied out of future production to the financier, and the financier receives the production payment in exchange for cash to the seller. The transaction is designed to obtain the most favorable tax results for both purchaser and seller.

Bottom-Hole Contribution. A *test-well contribution* which by agreement is required regardless of the outcome of the test well.

Carried Interest. The party to a *carried-interest arrangement* who is advanced development costs.

Carried-Interest Arrangement. An arrangement in which one owner (the *carrying interest*) agrees to advance development costs for another (the *carried interest*). Amounts advanced are recoverable only from the carried interest's share of future production. If the carried interest is paid out, it reverts to full working interest participation in which it bears a share of both production and further development costs and output.

Carrying Interest. The party to a *carried-interest arrangement* who advances development costs.

Carved-Out Production Payments. Sales or other commitments of a portion of minerals-in-place, particularly gas and oil, in advance of production. The seller is obligated to pay all production costs, but has no obligation to complete the payment if recoverable reserves prove insufficient. These arrangements are made as a means of financing the purchase of reserves or of maximizing the effect of allowable reductions in federal income taxes.

Delay Rentals. Additional rental payments which are required of a lessee if specified work on the leased property is not carried out within certain time periods.

Developed Reserves. In the petroleum industry, the amount of crude oil or natural gas that can be produced from existing facilities. Corresponds with "proven" reserves in the other mining industries.

Development. One of the five *extractive processes*. Development prepares a mineral discovery for commercial production.

Dry-Hole Contribution. A *test-well contribution* which by agreement is required only when the test well is unsuccessful.

Exploration. One of the five *extractive processes*. Exploration probes an area of probable mineralization for specific deposits. Commonly used to include geological and geophysical costs of *prospecting* nature.

Extractive Processes. *Prospecting*, acquisition, *exploration*, *development*, and production.

Farm-In Arrangement. A *farm-out arrangement* from the point of view of the second party.

Farm-Out Arrangement. An arrangement in the petroleum industry in which the owner or lessee of mineral rights (the first party) contracts them to another operator (the second party) for exploration and development. The first party retains an overriding royalty or other type of economic interest. The second party receives an assignment of mineral rights in exchange for undertaking to drill wells.

Free Well. A well drilled and equipped in exchange for a fractional part of the working interest.

Full-Cost Concept. A concept which regards companywide activities as one prospect. Based on this concept, costs of all *geological and geophysical studies*, all exploration costs, and all development costs are capitalized regardless of result and attributed to whatever minerals are found by the company.

Geological and Geophysical Studies. Processes which seek surface or subterranean indications of earth structure or formations of a type where experience has shown the possibility of mineral deposits.

IDC. Intangible drilling and development costs in the petroleum industry. Comprise expenses in preparing well locations, drilling and deepening wells, and preparing wells for initial production, none of which, because of their nature, has salvage value. Such expenditures would include labor, transportation, consumable supplies, drilling tool rentals, site clearance, and similar costs.

Lease Bonus. The amount paid the lessor as consideration for signing a lease, over and above any rental and royalty payments.

Lease Extension Costs. Additional amounts paid to extend lease beyond original term.

Lifting Costs. The costs associated with the operation of a well, usually including depreciation and amortization.

Mineral Right. The ownership of the minerals beneath the surface of the ground with the right to remove them. Mineral rights may be conveyed separately from surface rights.

Probable Reserves. In mining industries other than petroleum, the amount of reserves estimated to be available once additional development expenditures are incurred.

Production Payment. The right to a fraction of production or proceeds therefrom until a definite sum of money or a specified quantity of minerals has been received.

Profit-Sharing Interests. Participations in whatever profit might result from operations. These arrangements, usually made in connection with the acquisition of properties, are distinguished from working interests in a mineral deposit by the absence of full participation in output and costs.

Prospecting. The search for geological information leading to acquisition of exploration rights in areas of probable mineralization.

Proved (or Proven) Reserves. In the petroleum industry, the amount of crude oil or natural gas that can be produced from operated and nonoperated acreage even though it requires additional development drilling. In the other mining industries, the amount of reserves that can be produced through existing facilities.

Receding Face Costs. Development costs incurred to maintain current production after the operating stage of a mine has been reached.

Retreat. During the mining operations pillars are left in place for removal after the operations have reached the extremities of the mine, and the mine is in retreat. Retreat operations involve the removal of track and other salvageable equipment, as well as the removal of the pillars that were left during advance operations.

Royalty. An interest retained by the owner in fee that gives the owner a right to a fractional share of production, free and clear of exploration, development, and operating expenditures.

Shooting Rights. Permission to conduct geological and geophysical activity only, without the option to acquire lease acreage.

Shut-In Royalties. Amounts paid to lessors as compensation for loss of income resulting from nonproduction of producible reserves.

Strip Mine. A mine in which the mineral is at or near the surface. After removing the overburden, the mineral is mined with surface equipment. The term strip mine is most usually used in connection with coal mines.

Taconite. Iron-bearing rock which can be mined or quarried by the open-pit method. It is crushed and the major noniron material removed before it is shipped.

Take-or-Pay Contract. An agreement in which a buyer of minerals agrees to take or pay for a minimum quantity each year. Usually, any amount paid in excess of the price of minerals taken is recoverable from future purchases in excess of minimum quantities.

Test-Well Contribution. An agreement to pay the owner of an adjacent tract for a portion of the cost of drilling an exploratory well on his property.

Unit of Production Method. A method of computing depletion, depreciation, or amortization based on quantities produced in relation to total estimated reserves.

Working (Operating) Interest. The interest in a mineral property which entitles the owner to the production from the property, usually subject to a royalty and sometimes to other nonoperating interests. A working interest permits the owner to explore, develop, and operate the property.

Selected Bibliography

The following references have been selected to provide both general information on extractive industry operations and specific information on major accounting practices.

The best single-source overall reference found is *Economics of the Mineral Industries* edited by Edward H. Robie and published in 1964 by The American Institute of Mining, Metallurgical, and Petroleum Engineers, Inc. Four chapters of particular interest to this research study are listed in appropriate sections below.

Extractive Operations

AMERICAN PETROLEUM INSTITUTE. *Petroleum Facts and Figures,* 1965 and 1967 editions.

> *A comprehensive statistical presentation of operating data for the petroleum industry.*

AMERICAN PETROLEUM INSTITUTE, INDEPENDENT PETROLEUM ASSOCIATION OF AMERICA, AND MID-CONTINENT OIL & GAS ASSOCIATION. *Joint Association Survey (Section 2),* "Estimated Expenditures & Receipts of U. S. Oil and Gas Producing Industry." Department of Statistics, American Petroleum Institute, Washington, D.C. 1966.

BEHRE, CHARLES H., JR., and ARBITER, NATHANIEL, "Distinctive Features of the Mineral Industries," Chapter 2, pp. 43-79, *Economics of the Mineral Industries,* Edward H. Robie, editor. The American Institute of Mining, Metallurgical, and Petroleum Engineers, Inc. 1964.

BORDEN, GRANVILLE S. (updated by Frank H. Madison), "Taxation of Mineral Properties," Chapter 10, pp. 463-509, *Economics of the Mineral Industries,* Edward H. Robie, editor. The American Institute of Mining, Metallurgical, and Petroleum Engineers, Inc. 1964.

BOTTGE, ROBERT G., MCDIVITT, JAMES F., and MCCARL, HENRY N., "Prospecting for Natural Aggregates," *Rock Products*, May 1965, Part 1, pp. 108-115, 153-154, and June 1965, Part 2, pp. 92-95.

Methods of prospecting; sources of aggregates.

PRESTON, LEE E., *Exploration for Nonferrous Metals*. Resources for the Future, Inc. 1960.

The economic prospects of the nonferrous metal industries as they might affect public policy.

TYLER, PAUL M., CRANDALL, JOHN R., GLANVILLE, J. W., and COOKENBOO, L., "Cost of Acquiring and Operating Mineral Properties," Chapter 5, pp. 167-243, *Economics of the Mineral Industries*, Edward H. Robie, editor. The American Institute of Mining, Metallurgical, and Petroleum Engineers, Inc. 1964.

UNITED STATES DEPARTMENT OF THE INTERIOR, Bureau of Mines. *Metal-Mining Practice*, Bulletin 419. U.S. Government Printing Office. 1939.

Description of specific mining practices under various conditions from prospecting to sale of product. Includes unit costs of the various elements of operations experienced in many mines.

UNITED STATES DEPARTMENT OF THE INTERIOR, Bureau of Mines. *Mineral Facts and Problems*, Bulletin 585. U.S. Government Printing Office. 1960.

A general treatise on the characteristics, problems and position of metals, minerals and mineral fuels with particular reference to supply and demand factors. Comprehensive bibliographies are included.

UNITED STATES DEPARTMENT OF THE INTERIOR, Bureau of Mines. *Minerals Yearbook*, Vols. I-IV. U.S. Government Printing Office. 1967.

Various statistical data on mining activities.

UNITED STATES STEEL CORPORATION. *The Making, Shaping and Treating of Steel*, Seventh Edition. 1957.

Contains comprehensive discussion on methods of recovering coal and iron ore.

UNITED STATES TREASURY DEPARTMENT, Internal Revenue Service. *Statistics of Income . . . 1960, Supplemental Report*, "Depletion Allowance for Mineral Production Reported on U. S. Tax Returns." U. S. Government Printing Office. 1966.

YOUNG, GEORGE J., *Elements of Mining*, Third Edition, McGraw-Hill Book Company, Inc. 1932.

A detailed technical description of mining engineering principles.

Accounting

AMERICAN PETROLEUM INSTITUTE. *Report of Certain Petroleum Industry Accounting Practices.* 1965.

AMERICAN PETROLEUM INSTITUTE. *Report on Certain Petroleum Industry Accounting Practices,* Resurvey as of December 31, 1966. 1967.

ARTHUR ANDERSEN & Co. *Accounting for Oil and Gas Exploration Costs.* (Privately printed.) 1963.

An exposition of full-cost accounting.

BARTRAM, JOHN G., "The Cost of Finding Oil." University of Tulsa. *Accounting Papers of the Sixth Annual Conference of Accountants.* 1952, pp. 9-14.

A good discussion of the problems of relating exploration costs to discoveries and suggestions for evaluation of exploration department results.

BROCK, HORACE R., "Petroleum Accounting," *The Journal of Accountancy,* Dec. 1956, pp. 53-67.

The results of a survey on accounting for exploration and development costs and disposition of capitalized costs.

COUTTS, W. B., *Accounting Problems in the Oil and Gas Industry.* The Canadian Institute of Chartered Accountants. 1963.

FERNALD, HENRY B., PELOUBET, MAURICE E., and NORTON, LEWIS M., "Accounting for Nonferrous Metal Mining Properties and Their Depletion," *The Journal of Accountancy,* Aug. 1939, pp. 105-116.

GRADY, PAUL, *Accounting Research Study No. 7,* "Inventory of Generally Accepted Accounting Principles for Business Enterprises." American Institute of Certified Public Accountants. 1965.

IRVING, ROBERT H., and DRAPER, VERDEN R., *Accounting Practices in the Petroleum Industry.* The Ronald Press Company. 1958.

LEGION, WALTER A., "Special Features of Petroleum Accounting," Chapter 9, Part 2, pp. 450-462, *Economics of the Mineral Industries,* Edward H. Robie, editor. The American Institute of Mining, Metallurgical, and Petroleum Engineers, Inc. 1964.

NATIONAL ASSOCIATION OF COST ACCOUNTANTS. *Research Series No. 31,* "Costing Joint Products." 1957.

PELOUBET, MAURICE E., "Accounting for the Extractive Industries," Chapter 9, Part 1, pp. 403-450, *Economics of the Mineral Industries,* Edward H.

Robie, editor. The American Institute of Mining, Metallurgical, and Petroleum Engineers, Inc. 1964.

Peloubet, Maurice E., "Natural Resource Assets—Their Treatment in Accounts and Valuation," *Harvard Business Review*, Autumn 1937.

A treatise on the merits and limitations of statistical and financial data provided shareholders as a means of evaluating mining companies, particularly nonferrous metals. Includes a comparative review of movement in stock prices of two groups of companies, one recording depletion and one not recording depletion.

Pennsylvania Institute of Certified Public Accountants. "Accounting for the Coal Mining Industry," *Pennsylvania CPA Spokesman*, Aug. 1967.

Porter, Stanley P., *Petroleum Accounting Practices*. McGraw-Hill Book Company, Inc. 1965.

Includes illustration of effect of alternative practices on financial statements.

Smith, C. Aubrey, and Brock, Horace R., *Accounting for Oil Gas Producers*. Prentice-Hall, Inc. 1959.

Sonkin, Harry, "Sand and Gravel," Vol. V, Section 58, pp. 1649-1664, *Encyclopedia of Accounting Systems*, Robert I. Williams and Lillian Doris, editors. Prentice-Hall, Inc. 1957.